Legends and Truth about Ukraine

Olga Bandura

Published by Olha Bandura, 2023.

LEGENDS AND TRUTH ABOUT UKRAINE

First edition. December 26, 2023.

ISBN: 979-8224518500

Written by Olga Bandura.

The book is about unknown interesting facts about Ukraine!

Keep fighting – you are sure to win!
God helps you in the fight!
For flame and freedom march with you,
And right is on your side!
And on the renovated land
There'll be no enemy, no rival,
There will be son and will be the mother!
There will be people on the land!
Taras Shevchenko

Chapter One
Ukraine's Rich History and Legends

In the heart of Eastern Europe lies a land steeped in mystery, a country that echoes with the whispers of ancient tales and the resilient spirit of its people. Welcome to "Legends and Truth about Ukraine," an enthralling journey that unravels the captivating tapestry of a nation shrouded in both myth and reality.

As you embark on this literary adventure, prepare to be spellbound from the very first line. Imagine standing on the crossroads of history, where legends come alive and truth emerges from the depths of time. Ukraine, a land rich in cultural heritage, bears witness to stories that have shaped its identity and captivated the imaginations of generations.

The narrative unfolds like an ancient manuscript, each page revealing a new chapter in Ukraine's extraordinary narrative. From the mythical origins of Kyiv, the city of golden domes, to the hauntingly beautiful Carpathian Mountains, this Book invites you to explore the enigmatic corners of a country that has been a crossroads of civilizations for centuries.

But this is not just a collection of fables; it's a meticulous exploration of the veracity behind the myths. Through the lens of history, folklore, and modern insight, "Legends and Truth about Ukraine" unveils the layers of reality that interweave with the threads of legend. Discover the tales that have shaped the national psyche and gain a deeper understanding of Ukraine's complex and vibrant tapestry.

As you turn the pages, you'll encounter legendary heroes, mystical creatures, and epic battles that have left an indelible mark on the Ukrainian landscape. Yet, beneath the surface, you'll find the pulse of a nation pulsating with resilience, courage, and an unwavering determination to forge its destiny.

This Book is not just a mere recounting of events; it's an invitation to immerse yourself in the essence of Ukraine, a land where history and myth converge to create a narrative that is as intriguing as it is compelling. Join us as we navigate the corridors of time, separating fact from fiction, and unlocking the secrets that make Ukraine a treasure trove of legends and truths. Get ready to be captivated, for the journey is about to begin.

Chapter Two
Ancient times history
Legend of Kyiv.

A monument to founders of Kyiv

Once upon a time there lived three brave siblings - Kyi, Khoriv, and Schek, along with their spirited sister, Lybid.

One day they were boating along beautiful banks of the Dnieper. They saw three green hills covered with a thick forest. Kyi spoke with awe, "What a wonderful place!

"Let us settle here".

Kyi was the eldest brother. He was a tall handsome man with dark eyes and black hair. Kyi was very strong and clever. He made fine boats. Kyi loved the river and spent much time on the Dnieper.

Shchek, his younger brother, had green eyes and red hair. He was a good potter and he made fine jugs.

Khoryv, the youngest brother, had brown eyes and fair hair. He was a fine psaltery- player and sang beautiful songs. And he also made fine silver rings and other things.

Their sister Lybid was a pretty girl with blue eyes and long golden hair. She was very kind and modest. The three brothers loved their sister very much and took care of her. Kyi made a fine boat for Lybid and often brought her fish. Shchek presented Lybid with his best jugs. Khoryv made the most beautiful rings for his sister. Lybid loved her brothers and she wove snow-white linen for their shirts.

With Schek's unwavering strength, Khoriv's keen intellect, Kyi's steadfast leadership, and Lybid's unwavering spirit, they set about their monumental task. They gathered stones, shaped wood, and worked with unrelenting determination, each contributing their unique strengths to the noble cause.

Through laughter, sweat, and unwavering determination, the city began to take shape. Kyi, addressed the people who had gathered to witness this monumental creation. " This city, forged by our hands and fueled by our dreams, shall henceforth be known as Kyiv!"

As the sun dipped below the horizon, casting a golden glow upon the newly built city, the people rejoiced, celebrating the birth of Kyiv. Dancing, singing, and merry-making filled the air.

In the midst of the festivities, Lybid gazed upon the city with pride, whispering to her siblings, "Our legacy shall endure through the ages!"

For a long time, the people lived happily, but one day the enemies came to their land. They wanted to make the people their slaves. But the people didn't want to be slaves and they began to fight with their enemies.

The three brothers fought bravely and killed many enemies. At last Kyi took the chief of the enemies into his hands and threw him into the Dnieper. It was the end of the enemy.

After that Kyi became the first Prince of this land. The people built the first walled town on one of the hills at the river Dnieper and named it Kyiv in honour of their Prince.

Chapter Three
Legend about Ascold and Dir

Vikings

The legendary figures of Askold and Dir are often associated with the early history of Kyiv (Kiev), the capital of modern-day Ukraine.

According to one version of the legend, Askold and Dir were Varangian (Scandinavian) warriors who, along with their retinue, traveled southward through Eastern Europe in the 9th century. Eventually, they reached the region around the Dnieper River, where they encountered the Slavic tribes. The local Slavic people invited Askold and Dir to rule over them, and the Varangians established themselves as leaders in the area that would later become Kyiv.

"They asked Rurik to go to Constantinople with his kin, and both set out along the Dnieper. As they passed by, they saw a town on a hill and asked, 'Whose town is this?' The local residents replied, 'There were three brothers, Kiy, Shchek, and Khoriv, who built this town and perished. We now dwell in their town and pay tribute to the Khazars.' So, Askold and Dir remained in this town together, gathered many Varangians, and began to rule over the land of the Polyanians. Meanwhile, Rurik ruled in Novgorod."Askold and Dir became rulers of Kyiv and were said to have played significant roles in the early political and social development of the region".

In subsequent retellings and adaptations, Askold and Dir have become legendary figures symbolizing the early Varangian influence in the region and the establishment of Kyiv as a significant political center. Their story is often romanticized, and various interpretations exist in literature, art, and folklore.

In 882, Askold and his forces were killed after the siege of Kiev by the Novgorod army led by Oleg. This event marked the beginning of the rule of the Rurik dynasty, which lasted for about 500 years and extended its influence from Galicia to Moscow.

Under Askold, Kyiv gradually becomes a political center with adjacent lands of the Polians, Derevlians, Dregovichs, and the southwestern part of the Severyans. The main interests of Askold's Rus covered the south and southeast. It was attracted to rich and powerful states such as the Khazars, Bulgaria, Byzantium, as well as Georgia, Armenia, and even distant Baghdad. With them, it maintained active trade and political ties."

The Varangians, Askold and Dir, are figures from Slavic and Norse legends and historical accounts. The Varangians were a group of warriors, traders, and adventurers from Scandinavia who played a significant role in Eastern European history. Askold and Dir are often mentioned together in the context of early East Slavic history and the establishment of the Kievan Rus.

Chapter Four
Princess Olga

Princess Olga

Once upon a time, in the ancient city of Kyiv, there ruled a wise and just princess named Olga. She was known far and wide for her intelligence, kindness, and unmatched leadership. Her kingdom prospered under her rule, and the people loved her dearly.

Princess Olga was not only a wise ruler but also a compassionate one. She would often spend her days walking through the streets of Kyiv, talking to her subjects and ensuring that everyone in the kingdom was content. One day, as she strolled through the bustling marketplace, she overheard a group of children talking about a magical forest on the outskirts of the city.

Intrigued by the tales of this enchanted forest, Princess Olga decided to explore it herself. She gathered a group of loyal knights, and together they embarked on a journey into the mysterious woods. As they ventured deeper, the air became filled with an otherworldly energy, and the trees whispered secrets of times long past.

After a day of exploration, Princess Olga and her knights stumbled upon a clearing bathed in golden light. In the center of the clearing stood a magnificent tree with silver leaves that sparkled like stars. As they approached, the tree began to speak in a gentle, melodic voice.

"Welcome, Princess Olga, to the Heartwood Grove," said the tree. "I am the Guardian of the Forest, and I have been awaiting your arrival."

Princess Olga, amazed by the magical presence of the Guardian, asked, "Why have you been waiting for me?"

The Guardian explained that the magic of the forest was connected to the well-being of the kingdom. Over the years, the balance had been disrupted, and only a wise and just ruler like Princess Olga could restore harmony.

Determined to fulfill her duty, Princess Olga sought the guidance of the Guardian. Together, they devised a plan to bring prosperity and happiness back to the kingdom. Princess Olga returned to Kyiv with newfound wisdom, and under her leadership, the kingdom flourished like never before.

The enchanted forest and the Heartwood Grove became a symbol of Princess Olga's reign, a reminder of the magic that can be found in wisdom, kindness, and just rule. And so, the tale of Princess Olga of Kyiv and the magical forest became a cherished story passed down through generations, inspiring rulers and citizens alike to value wisdom, justice, and the well-being of their kingdom.

She was the eminent Kyiv princess, the first Christian governess of Kyiv Rus and the first Ukrainian canonized saint. Some consider the princess Olga as a one of the cruelest and the most imperious rulers, while others think of her as a perfect mother, faithful wife and the wisest woman in Kyiv Rus history. So, what do we know about this princess who was respected by all men and who gained the throne of ancient Kyiv Rus?

According to the chronicles, Olga was born around 894 near Pskov. There are few versions about her origin. Some historians think that she was a daughter of the famous prince Prophetic Oleg and she inherited his gift of prophecy. Other say that she had Scandinavian origins and her real name was Helga.

In 903, Olga was given in marriage to Igor, the son of Ryurik, the future great prince, who was 25 years old in that time. The legend says that Igor and Olga occasionally met in the forest where the young prince was hunting. He was impressed by intelligence, beauty and independent behavior of Olga.

Life with Igor

Igor became a full-fledged ruler of Kyiv Rus at the age of 35. Olga, who was already a grown-up woman, was a faithful and loving wife. Their mutual love gave birth to Sviatoslav, who was destined to become one of the most powerful Kyiv princes, known under the name Sviatoslav the Brave. Igor often left home to take part in distant war battles, so in these periods Olga was involved in the actual ruling of the state. Igor had to fight with nomads, and the worst of them were Drevlians tribe that regularly violated borders of Kyiv Rus and ravaged the country by cruel raids.

Revenge for the Murder of her Husband

One of the most famous legends surrounding Princess Olga is the story of her revenge for the murder of her husband, Igor I of Kyiv. According to the Primary Chronicle, after Igor's death, Olga took vengeance on the Drevlians, the tribe responsible for his murder.

The revenge involved a complex and brutal scheme, including the burning of the Drevlian leaders in a bathhouse. This tale is often cited as an example of Olga's cunning and determination.

The chronicles say that the prince Igor died in the battle with Drevlians in 945 after numerous attempts to levy tributes from them.

That time, Olga was waiting for her husband to come back from war, but she experienced terrible dreams and signs and felt that Igor was killed. Unfortunately, her intuition did not lie to her.

The warriors that returned from the battle gave her Igor`s sword and told her that he fell in a battle. Drevlians murdered Igor in a very violent way – they ripped his body in half.

The prince Sviatoslav was only three years old, so the princess Olga became the actual ruler of Kyiv Rus and the representative of rightful heir of the throne. Igor`s troops accepted her new status, appreciating her strong will, intellect and wisdom.

Right after the death of Igor, Drevlians sent affiancers to Olga, proposing her to marry their prince Mal. 20 affiancers came in the boat. Olga ordered her men to carry the boat with Drevlians to her yard and throw it into a deep pit that had been specially dug there in advance. After that, Drevlians were buried in that pit alive together with their boat.

Then Olga asked Drevlians to send her another affiancers – the most noble and high-powered ones. The Drevlians, who thought that maybe the princess could change her mind, accepted her request.

However, it was not the best decision for them: the envoys were burned alive by Olga in a bath while they were washing up preparing for a meeting with the princess.

After these events, the princess have come to the land of Drevlians with a small group of troops to hold a traditional funeral feast on the grave of her husband Igor. The insidious princess gave Drevlians too much to drink, and after they fell asleep, she ordered her warriors to hack them to death. The chronicles say that 5 000 Drevlians were killed on that day.

After the massacre, Olga came again to Drevlian`s lands with her army in 946. The Drevlians took shelter in their city Iskorosten that had strong defense fortifications. Then Olga used again her brilliant mind to cheat the enemies. She promised them to drop back if she received a pigeon as a tribute from every home of Iskorosten. When Drevlians accepted her conditions, the princess tied smoldering wood splinters to the legs of each bird, and then let pigeons free. The birds flied back to their homes, so the city burnt to ashes. Victorious Olga passed through the land of Drevlians and imposed tributes and taxes all over it. Then she returned to Kyiv.

Conversion to Christianity

Another legend surrounds Princess Olga's conversion to Christianity. It is said that she was baptized in Constantinople and became a fervent Christian. This conversion is considered significant in the history of Kyivan Rus as it laid the groundwork for the later Christianization of the region.

The princess Olga became the first governess of Kyiv Rus who was Christianized, while all her warriors and people were still pagans. Olga wanted to unite people with some great idea, and decided that Christian religion might be a good choice. Besides, she understood that she needed new connections, enforcing her power and support from other mighty states. Therefore, in 955 Olga paid a visit to Constantinople. In Constantinople, she was Christianized and given Christian name Elena.

There is an interesting story behind this event. The Byzantine emperor Constantine VII Porphyrogennetos was so charmed by outstanding personality and beauty of Olga that he decided to propose her. But Olga was a pagan, so it was impossible to arrange a marriage. The solution was obvious: Olga had to become a Christian. Olga accepted this, and Constantine personally performed the ceremony of her Christianizing.

However, then smart Olga, who did not plan to marry the emperor, said that they could not get married because she was not allowed to become a wife of her godfather. The emperor, impressed by her contrivance, gifted Olga valuable treasures and sent her home. In such a way, the princess Olga has achieved all her goals: the Byzantine Empire got aware about Kyiv Rus and began to support it. The fact that Olga was now a Christian became the guarantee of the emperor`s grace.

Miraculous Healing Spring

There is a legend that a spring with healing properties appeared where Olga was baptized. Pilgrims would come to this spring seeking healing, and it was believed to have miraculous properties.

Ascension to Heaven: In some folk tales, Princess Olga is depicted as ascending to heaven in a fiery chariot, symbolizing her holiness and eventual sainthood.

The period of Olga`s rule became a decisive turn in the history of Kyiv Rus. The country received a well-organized government and began to integrate into political system of the Christian world. Olga built monasteries and churches in Kyiv Rus and preached Christ.

Grand Princess Olga of Kyiv was also renowned for building many important edifices. The Joachim Chronicles mention the construction of the wooden church of St. Sofia in the Kyiv Acropolis. The "Tale of Bygone Years" also refers to the great Kyiv Palace of Princess Olga.

Princess Olga first set to cleaning up the tribute system: she established certain norms for taxes and brought in new terminology and practices, such as "устави, уроки, дані" (statutes, classes, data) that were recorded by chroniclers. Tribute collected from the Drevlians and other tribes was divided into three parts: two went to Kyiv, and the third – to Vyshhorod, where Olga had her residence.

Princess Olga introduced laws for industrial hunting of fur-bearing animals and specified which areas were to provide fur to the state treasury. Subordinated tribes also gave fur as tribute to the central state, and was in great demand in other European countries.

She was even canonized by the Christian church as a saint. Nestor the Chronicler mentioned her as harbinger of the Christian era in Kyiv Rus and called her "Predawn star".

The list of Olga`s achievements in the period of her governing is very long. Olga paid much attention to development, beautification and defense of Kyiv: she built a new residence "Olga`s yard" with stone tower, wooden Christian church and a system of reliable fortifications in the capital. Domestic policy measures taken by Olga helped to unite former tribal lands into one powerful state.

As for external policy, Olga preferred diplomacy to war. In 957, she signed agreement with Constantine VII Porphyrogennetos; according to this agreement, she sent her warriors to help the Byzantine Empire in its wars with Arabs, Northmen and Bulgarians. She also made the first attempt to establish diplomatic connection with Western Europe. In 959, she sent envoys to the German emperor Otto I with the request to assign a bishop for Christianization of Kyiv Rus. However, the Christian mission of German bishop Adalbert, that took place in 961-962, became a failure. Olga truly wished to Christianize her people, but she did not achieve this goal. Only her grandson, Volodymyr, Christianized Kyiv Rus in 988.

The princess Olga died around 969, leaving behind a great contribution to the history and development of Kyiv Rus in the X century. This brave and wise woman managed not only to retain the power in her land, but also reinforced it, and generally improved the image of Kyiv Rus in the whole world.

Chapter Five
Kyiv gave Europe 158 queens and kings.

Queen Anna

Before you stands a historical portrayal - a portrait of Queen Anna (about a thousand years ago), captured in the Hagia Sophia Cathedral in Kiev. This portrait is the work of Ukrainian artist Volodymyr Kozyuk, who created it using artificial intelligence (AI), based on the original portrait of the princess in the Hagia Sophia Cathedral in Kiev.

In this temple, all the famous queens of Europe of Ukrainian origin are depicted: Anna of France, Anastasia of Hungary, Elizabeth of Norway and Denmark, and Agatha of England. All four are daughters of Yaroslav the Wise, the Grand Prince of Kiev. The entire Europe had familial ties with Kiev, Russia, present-day Ukraine! And all this happened 100 years before the establishment of the "village" of Moscow.

Let's go back to the Ukrainian queens; each of their stories could potentially be adapted into a Hollywood movie! Did you know that the recently deceased Queen Elizabeth of England was a descendant of the Ukrainian queen Agata?

Margaret of Scotland (1045–1093), the daughter of Agatha Yaroslavna and King Edward (the Exile) of England, became the Queen of Scotland. She was canonized by Pope Innocent IV in 1250 and was included in the list of saints. In 1673, Margaret was declared the heavenly patroness of Scotland. She is also known as the patron saint of large families, Catholic households, and the patron of the University of Edinburgh.

The legendary Anna of Kyiv, who became the Queen of France, spoke four languages. She carried the Gospel, on which almost all subsequent kings of France swore their oaths, and it was written and printed in Kyiv. Ukrainian blood of Queen Anna flowed through the veins of more than 18 kings of France.

The daughter of Princess of Kyivan Rus-Ukraine Anna Yaroslavna and King of France Henry I, Emma, became Saint Edigna of Ukrainian Greek Catholic and Roman Catholic Churches in Europe. Another granddaughter of Yaroslav the Wise, Margaret of Scotland, the daughter of Queen Consort of England Agatha Yaroslavna, was also canonized.

About Saint Edith:

Emma, the daughter of a French monarch from the Capetian dynasty and a Ukrainian princess from the Rurikid dynasty, was born in Paris in the year 1055. She later became the queen of France. The couple also had sons: Philip I (who would become the future king of France), Hugh (who became the Count of Vermandois and Valois and played a role in the First Crusade), and Robert (who died in childhood).

"Very beautiful granddaughter of the Grand Prince of Kiev, Yaroslav the Wise, received a good education at the French court. Around the year 1074, nineteen-year-old Emma fled from the royal court, rejecting an arranged marriage," writes Dr. Taras Chukhlib, a historian from Ukraine.

The girl was planning to reach Kiev, about which she had heard so much from Anna Yaroslavna, her mother. According to legend, on the way, Emma had a dream that became prophetic for her: she must stay forever where, while leaving on a "telegraph," she would hear the simultaneous crowing of a rooster and the sound of a bell. And so, this prophecy came true near the village of Puch in Bavaria (approximately 30 km from the modern city of Munich in Germany).

The daughter of the King of France settled in the trunk of an old linden tree and lived there as a nun in a cell for over 30 years. She subsisted on only plant-based food, leading a pious lifestyle. She taught children to read and write, introducing them to Christian values.

"The preacher of the Christian faith discovered the healing gift of a local herbalist. For many years, she not only treated the local population but also livestock. The Ukrainian woman actively assisted people in overcoming illnesses and adversity," recounts the historian when speaking of legends.

The fame of the beauty and miraculous healer Emma, whom the Germans baptized as Edigna, spread throughout Bavaria and later across Europe. During her lifetime, a temple was erected by a lime tree, and in this temple, the blessed woman who passed away on February 26, 1109, was later laid to rest. Grateful peasants buried her in the altar of the local church.

Let's note that we learned about the high origin of the healer only after her death. In the year 1600, the Roman Catholic Church declared Edigna blessed.

Photo: Edigna in the lime tree. 18th-century ceiling fresco, St. Sebastian's Church in Puch, Gerany.

Let's remind the Hungarians about their Ukrainian queen, Anastasia. Thanks to the mediation of Kiev and its powerful princes, the Hungarian king Andros, husband of Anastasia, was saved from death! At that time, Kiev Rus was the largest state in Europe with the strongest influence!

Another granddaughter of Yaroslav the Wise, recognized as a saint, is Margaret of Scotland. It is worth noting that she was also recognized as a saint by the Catholic Church in Europe. Margaret was yet another granddaughter of Yaroslav the Wise, who, interestingly, had all four of his daughters marry kings and monarchs of Norway, France, Hungary, and England. The descendants of these marriages later became European monarchs.

Margaret of Scotland (1045-1093), the daughter of Agatha Yaroslavna and King Edward (the Exile) of England, became the Queen of Scotland. She was canonized by Pope Innocent IV in 1250. In 1673, Margaret was declared the heavenly patroness of Scotland. She is also referred to as the patroness of large families and Catholic households, as well as the patron of the University of Edinburgh.

Photo: Image of Saint Margaret in Edinburgh.

By the way, the daughter of Margaret and the Scottish king Malcolm III, Matilda (Edith), became the wife of the King of England, Henry I, and among her direct descendants was Richard the Lionheart.

Matilda Scottish

Anna Yaroslavna

Queen Anna

She was also known as Anne of Kyiv, a queen consort of France.

She was born around 1024 in Kyiv, which is now the capital of Ukraine. Anna was the daughter of Yaroslav the Wise, Grand Prince of Kyiv, and Ingegerd Olofsdotter of Sweden.

At this time, all of Rus was literate. Let us recall at least the birch bark letters of this year, of which many have been found. Anna is the youngest of the three daughters of the Kyiv prince Yaroslav the Wise, the wife of the French king Henry I and the queen of France. Anna grew up at the prince's court and received a good education.

The name of the daughter of the great Kyivan prince Yaroslav Volodymyrovych the Wise, Anna, has always sparked considerable interest among scholars and anyone interested in the history of Kyivan Rus. Anna's childhood years were spent in Kyiv, growing up in the splendid and picturesque ancient city. Today, it is the old part of the city with many outstanding architectural structures. Anna's childhood coincided with a tumultuous period of political and cultural life in the state.

This was a period of general cultural flourishing in Rus at the beginning of the 11th century. In addition to lavish banquets, hunting, and church services typical of the ancient world, Kyiv under Yaroslav the Wise stood out for its active civic and educational life. Schools were established, libraries were founded, and the copying and translation of books were important state matters. At the prince's court, evenings reminiscent of modern literary and vocal events took place, where poets, musicians, and jesters performed.

Thus, Anna grew up in a cultural atmosphere in a state that was considered one of the most powerful and advanced in the world at that time.

Private tutors taught the princess literacy, history, foreign languages, singing, drawing, and etiquette. It can be assumed that the choice of the French king Henry I, who sought the hand of Anna Yaroslavna, was influenced not only by political considerations: the fame of the beauty and intelligence of the Rus princess spread throughout Europe, reaching France as well.

Henry I and Anna

In 1051, Anna married King Henry I of France. She became Queen of France and played a significant role in the French court.

During the coronation that took place in the Cathedral of Reims, Anna presented the Gospel brought from Kyiv. Upon ascending the French throne, all subsequent kings swore their oaths on this Gospel, likely unaware of its origin from Kyiv. Researchers note that the intellect of this remarkable woman impressed the French. In one of the letters to Anna, Pope Nicholas II wrote appreciating her virtue, royal dignity, and respect for the church.

However, her marriage faced challenges, and after the death of her husband in 1060, she struggled to maintain influence and protect the interests of her sons.

Anna Yaroslavna is notable for her role as a regent for her son, King Philip I of France, during his minority. She faced political intrigues and conflicts within the royal court. Her efforts to maintain stability and protect her family's interests were crucial during a tumultuous period in French history.

It's important to note that Anna Yaroslavna was not a queen regnant (ruling queen) but a queen consort, meaning she was the wife of a reigning king. The title "queen of France" is often used to refer to a queen consort.

One legend that has been associated with Anna Yaroslavna involves her journey to France. According to some accounts, Anna faced opposition from the French court due to cultural differences and her Eastern European background. The legend tells of how Anna, feeling isolated and homesick, turned to prayer for guidance. In response, she dreamt of Saint Genevieve, the patron saint of Paris, who assured her that she would find favor in her new homeland and play a crucial role in shaping the destiny of France.

Another aspect of the legend might involve Anna's influence on French culture. She is said to have introduced certain Eastern customs and traditions to the French court, enriching the cultural tapestry of medieval France. This cultural exchange between East and West could be portrayed as a magical or transformative force in the legend.

Letter from the Queen of France Anna Yaroslavna to her father in Kiev Rus. Impression of Paris.

Anna Yaroslavna Rurikovich - Queen of France.

"Hello, my dear darling! Your faithful daughter Anechka, Anna Yaroslavna Rurikovich, who is now the French queen, is writing to you, the prince of all Kiev Rus. And where did you send me, a sinner? Into the stinking hole, to France, to the Paris-town, be it wrong! You said: the French are smart people, but they don't even know the stove. As soon as winter begins, we heat the fireplace. There is soot through the whole palace, smoke in the whole hall, but there is not a drop of heat. Only Russian beavers and sables are here to save myself. Once I called their masons, and began to explain what a stove is. She drew, drew blueprints for them - they would name science, and that's it. "Madam," they say, "that's impossible." I answer: "Do not be lazy, go to Russia, we have a stove in every wooden hut, not like in stone chambers." And they told me: "Madam, we do not believe. So that there was a closet with fire in the house, and there was no fire? Oh, non-non! " I swore to them.

They say: "You, Russes, are barbarians, Scythians, Asians, this is your witchcraft. Look, madam, do not tell anyone but us, otherwise they will burn you and me at the stake! " And they eat, you know what? You won't believe - frogs! Even ordinary people in our country would be ashamed to take such things into their mouths, but they have dukes and duchesses who eat and praise them at the same time. They also eat cutlets. They will take a piece of meat, beat it with a hammer, fry it and eat it. Their Byzantine spoons are still news, and they have never seen Venetian forks. I once took and cooked a chicken for my spouse, King Henry. He licked his hands straight. "Anchor! - shouts. - Still!" I cooked him some more. He will shout again: "Anchor!" I told him: "The stomach hurts!" He: "Kes-kyo-se? - What it is?" I explained to him about Claudius Galen.

He says: "You are a warlock! Look, don't tell anyone, otherwise the Pope will order us to burn at the stake". Another time I said to Henry: "Let me teach your fools to stage Alexandria." He: "What is it?" I say: "The history of the wars of Alexander the Great." "Who is he?" Well, I explained to him about Antisthenes the Younger. He told me: "Oh, non-non! This is incredible! One person cannot conquer so many countries! " Then I showed him the book. He winced in disgust and said: "I am not a priest to read so much! In Europe, not a single king can read. Look who you don't show, otherwise my dukes and counts will quickly kill you with daggers! " This is the kind of life here, darling.

And the Saracens also came to us. No one, except me, speaks Saracenic rumor, the queen had to become a translator, even the dukes and counts were grinding their teeth. Yes, I am not afraid of this, my Varangians are always with me. Something else is scary. These Saracens invented alkugl (Arabic - alcohol), it is even stronger than our home brew and mead, not like Polish vodka. That's why I am writing to you, my dear, so that this alkohol does not come to Russia even a single barrel. Not God! Otherwise, the death will be for the Russian people. For this I bow to you forgiving, being your faithful daughter Anna Yaroslavna Rurikovich, and by her husband Anna Regina Francorum. "

Anna Yaroslavna carried out a revolution in a foreign country for herself. It was she who taught the French court to read and write in the 11th century. It was she who introduced the French to the bath and made them use cutlery while eating. Anna corresponded with the Pope. The subjects of France, foreign to her, idolized Anna and called her Red Agnes.

Anna Yaroslavna signed herself like this: "Anna Rina".

Facts indicate that the wife of King Henry I held a significant position in the French society of that time and actively participated in governing the state alongside her husband. In France, Anna promoted the traditions of respect for education, shaping the atmosphere and spirit of the society in which she spent her childhood and youth.

In the gloomy 1930s during Stalin's lawlessness when the Bolsheviks wanted to destroy the Saint Sophia Cathedral, French writer Romain Rolland met with Stalin in Moscow and defended the cathedral, stating that it should not be demolished if only because it was built by the father of the French queen, Yaroslav the Wise.

Queen Anna has forever left her mark on the history of France. She is our compatriot whom we have the right to be proud of, just as we take pride in many illustrious women on the generous Ukrainian land.

Cossak

Chapter Six
Cossackdom in the history of Ukraine

Cossackdom in the history of Ukraine has ancient roots and is defined not only as a military caste but also as a distinctive socio-cultural and political phenomenon. The main period of Cossack development in Ukraine spans the 16th to 18th centuries.

Early Period of Cossackhood (late 15th - early 16th century): The first mentions of Cossacks date back to the late 15th century when they served as mercenaries in military conflicts. Over time, they gained more autonomy and became a crucial element in defending the borders against attacks from the Turks and Crimean Tatars.

Zaporizhian Sich (late 16th - early 18th century): Founded in the mid-16th century on the island of Khortytsia in the Dnipro River, the Zaporizhian Sich became a center of Cossack self-governance. Zaporizhian Cossacks actively fought for freedom and independence, forming alliances with various countries, including Poland and Muscovy.

The Hetmanate (late 17th - early 18th century): In the 17th and 18th centuries, hetmans emerged as elected leaders of the Cossack army and prominent political figures. Hetmans recognized the authority of either the Ottoman Empire or the Russian state. The Hetmanate led to a loss of some autonomy for the Cossack community.

Gradual Decline (late 18th century - 19th century): Over time, Cossackdom lost its power and significance. Under the rule of the Russian Empire, Ukrainian Cossackdom became less autonomous, and the concept of a "Cossack" became less associated with military service.

Cossackdom played a significant role in shaping Ukraine's history, determining its fate, and contributing to its cultural identity. Modern Ukraine continues to honor the Cossack heritage as an important element of its national identity.

And again, about blood of Ukrainians. Baturyn massacre

Baturyn Massacre

"The fearsome Muscovite czar, bloodthirsty in Ukraine... All residents of Baturyn, regardless of age and gender, were slaughtered, as dictated by the inhumane customs of the Muscovites," reported the leading French newspaper "Gazette de France" in 1708.

On November 14, 1708, Moscow forces under the command of Prince Menshikov massacred 15,000 residents of the Hetmanate capital, the city of Baturyn, including women and children. In Ukrainian history, these events are known as the "Baturyn Massacre." The Moscow troops looted the city, including Orthodox churches, and subsequently, on Menshikov's orders, set it on fire, destroying the churches.

The destruction of Baturyn along with the civilian population was a tragedy not only for Ukraine but also on an international and European level. European newspapers of that time described the events in Baturyn as "A Terrible Massacre," "Women and Children on the Blades of Sabers," "All of Ukraine Bathes in Blood. Menshikov Shows the Horrors of Moscow's Atrocities." In the 18th century, Europe unequivocally perceived the Baturyn massacre as a war crime, a crime against civilian populations, and a crime against humanity, although such terms did not yet exist. They only emerged in the 20th century after the shocking atrocities of Russian Bolshevism, Nazis, and their followers – Ukrainian nationalists, executioners, and marauders.

"I was still a minor when glorious Moscow set Baturyn ablaze at night, killed Chechel, and drowned young and old in the Sejm. I lay among the corpses right in the chambers of Mazepa... Around me, my sister, and my mother were slain, embracing, lying with me..."

Taras Schevchenko

Cossack Colonel Ivan Bohun

Y. Madeevsky. Ivan Bogun. Lithography. 1884

Ivan Bohun is a historical figure, a prominent military leader, and commander who lived in the 17th century in the Polish-Lithuanian Commonwealth. He belonged to the nobility, and his father, Petro Bohun, was also a military figure. Ivan Bohun served in various military units of the Commonwealth and participated in many crucial battles, including wars against the Turks and Tatars.

However, his name became widely known due to events related to the Khmelnytsky Uprising of 1648-1654. In 1648, Ivan Bohun was elected colonel of the Chernihiv regiment and joined the insurgents under the command of Bohdan Khmelnytsky. However, in subsequent events, he showed his independence from the hetman, and in 1651, he refused to recognize the authority of Khmelnytsky. In 1651, Bohun, along with his regiment, joined the army of the Crown Hetman Mykola Potocki and took part in the Battle of Berestechko. However, in 1652, his regiment was defeated in the Battle of Baturyn.

Ivan Bohun is considered a national hero and a symbol of the struggle for the freedom of the Ukrainian people. His name is often mentioned in literature and art, as well as in the monuments of Ukraine's national history.

The speech of Cossack Colonel Ivan Bohun about Muscovy, delivered at the fateful Pereyaslav Council for Ukraine in 1654: "In Muscovy, the most abhorrent slavery prevails. There is nothing that can be considered one's own because everything belongs to the tsar. Muscovite boyars call themselves 'slaves of the tsar.' The entire Muscovite people are slaves. In Muscovy, they sell people in the market like cattle. Joining such a nation is worse than jumping into the fire alive..."

Bohdan Khmelnitsky

Bohdan Khmelnitsky, Hetman of the Zaporozhian Host

The parents of Bohdan Khmelnitsky were unknown and unseen by anyone. On the hill where the church now stands, there lived a grandfather and grandmother. Around them grew thick, dense hops.

The grandfather and grandmother had no children, and they were saddened by this.

One morning, the grandfather went out of the house and heard what seemed like a child's voice. He began to clear the hops with his hands and walked towards the source of the voice. In the thick hops, he found a boy. The child lay before him, and the sun shone in its head. The grandfather crossed himself, took the child, and carried it to the house, and the sun also went with him. As soon as the grandfather entered the house, he saw that the walls had parted, and in the place of the old house, palaces had grown, and in all the chambers, it became bright and clear.

The grandfather and grandmother named this child Bohdan Khmelnitsky. This was because they believed that God himself had sent them this child, and "Khmelnitsky" because they found the boy in the hops (khmel). Bohdan grew not by days, but by hours. Soon he grew up, and all the Cossacks gathered around him. Whatever he said, the Cossacks listened to him. Bohdan, with his Cossacks, built a church not far from his chambers, and he dug pits under the church to lead his horses to Tyasmin for water. When enemies attacked him, he and his Cossacks would retreat into these pits, and then unexpectedly emerge from there to defeat the enemies.

Hetman of the Zaporozhian Host, a talented military commander, and strategist, who achieved several significant victories that are etched in history. He led Ukrainian lands in a liberation war against the Polish-Lithuanian Commonwealth from 1648 to 1657. He declared that his goal was to free the entire Ukrainian people from Polish oppression and unite Ukrainian territories into an independent state. To withstand the Polish-Lithuanian Commonwealth and the Ottoman Empire, he signed the Treaty of Pereyaslav with Moscow in 1654, securing military support for Ukraine from Russia.

However, in making this agreement, the hetman did not anticipate the strategic defeat from the "embraces" of Moscow, which began to consider Ukrainian lands as its own, imposing its governors and systems, and appointing its own hetmans. Ultimately, after the death of Bohdan Khmelnytsky, a 30-year period of "Ruina" (1657-1687) began in Ukrainian territories. Ten hetmans after his death unsuccessfully attempted to rid Ukraine of Moscow's influence. Khmelnytsky died on August 6, 1657, in Chyhyryn, and he was buried in Subotiv, in the St. Elijah's Church, which was built with his funds.

The Constitution of Pylyp Orlyk

Pylyp Orlyk Hetman of the Zaporozhian Host

The Constitution of Pylyp Orlyk is a document of great significance in the history of Ukrainian statehood, being the first Ukrainian and one of the earliest European constitutions. It was written 66 years before the American Declaration of Independence and nearly 80 years before the French Declaration of the Rights of Man and of the Citizen. Until his last days, the Hetman tirelessly sought support for Ukrainian statehood from the rulers of France, Great Britain, the Vatican, Saxony, and Prussia. He drew the attention of European leaders to the tragic fate of his homeland, which was divided among voracious neighbors.

Pylyp Orlyk was a notable figure in Ukrainian history, particularly during the 17th century. Born in 1672 in a family of the Lithuanian nobility of Czech origin in what is now Belarus, his father died in battle against the Turks when Pylyp was just one year old. Raised by his mother, he received his education at the Kyiv-Mohyla Academy, which later gained the status of a college.

Historians highlight Pylyp 's rapid career growth, attributed to two main factors. Firstly, he gained the favor of Hetman Ivan Mazepa, becoming one of his closest associates. Pylyp was possibly one of the few individuals who knew about Mazepa's secret dealings with Polish politicians within the Polish-Lithuanian Commonwealth. Secondly, Pylyp Orlyk delved into the essence of international relations, deciphering the intricacies of the intrigues involving the key players in the Great Northern War – Russia, Sweden, and Poland.

Moreover, Pylyp Orlyk was an exceptionally educated person and demonstrated conscientiousness in his official duties. He engaged in tasks that involved understanding the complexities of international relations and unraveling the intrigues of the prominent actors in the Northern War. His knowledge spanned the political landscape of the time, involving Russia, Sweden, and Poland.

Pylyp Orlyk is particularly remembered for his role as a diplomat and advisor to Hetman Ivan Mazepa during a crucial period in Eastern European history, marked by geopolitical conflicts and shifting alliances.

The relationship between Ivan Mazepa and the Russian Tsar Peter was initially good. However, over time, Mazepa began to conceive a secret plan to create an independent Cossack state free from Moscow's influence. With each passing year, Peter increasingly disregarded the interests of Ukrainians, especially in terms of personal rights and freedoms, particularly those of the Cossacks. Mazepa defended these interests before the Tsar, but eventually made a difficult decision – openly declaring war against Peter and becoming an ally of the Swedish King Charles XII.

In April 1710, after Mazepa's death, the Cossacks who remained loyal to him elected Pylyp Orlyk as the Hetman of the Zaporozhian Host. Orlyk was immediately recognized by the Turkish Sultan and the Swedish King, with whom he agreed to continue the war against Russia. While in exile, Orlyk and his associates wrote the "Legal Code and Constitution Regarding the Rights and Freedoms of the Zaporozhian Host," considered the first Ukrainian constitution. It began with the words: **"Ukraine on both sides of the Dnieper must be free from foreign domination."**

It is hard to believe, but over 300 years ago, Orlyk foresaw the creation of a parliament. However, it was not intended to be called the Supreme Rada but the General Council. It was supposed to consist of the general elder, colonels, general advisors – representatives of Cossack regiments, regimental elders, sotniks, and representatives of the Zaporozhian Sich. To realize these rights and freedoms, there was only one thing left – to get rid of the tsarist "guardianship" and become a fully-fledged hetman of Ukraine. So, while in Moscow they bowed to the tsar, Ukraine had already laid the foundations of a sovereign, free, and civilized country. Glory to Ukraine!

Ivan Sirko

Hetman Ivan Sirko

Hetman Ivan Sirko (1605–1680) is a legendary figure in Ukrainian history. Ivan Sirko is one of the most well-known and controversial figures in the history of Ukrainian Cossacks.

The legend of being born with teeth. From the very moment the Cossack child was born, something seemed amiss. According to the legend, young Sirko was born with teeth. When the midwife saw this, her heart nearly stopped. She couldn't believe her eyes. She quickly spread the news throughout the village, declaring that a true werewolf had been born into the Sirko family.

The rumor quickly circulated, and the entire village became convinced that the child was a harbinger of danger. Old wise folks muttered, "This means he will spend his entire life biting enemies." The news of the unusual birth spread far and wide, and people couldn't help but speculate about the mystical qualities and challenges the child with teeth might bring to the community.

Despite the initial shock and fear, young Sirko grew up to be a strong and courageous individual, always proving himself in battles and challenges. The legend of his birth with teeth became a symbol of his unique destiny, and he embraced his unconventional start in life as he went on to become a legendary figure in Cossack folklore.

Sirko, who is referred to as "шайтан" (shaitan) or "чорт" (devil) by others. From childhood, Sirko exhibited unusual and seemingly supernatural abilities, such as turning into a wolf, catching bullets with his teeth, and engaging in other unnatural activities. Witnesses claimed to have seen him perform these feats.

Tatars, it is mentioned, called him "шайтан" (shaitan) or devil because they couldn't understand why they consistently lost battles to the audacious Ukrainian. However, it is also noted that even the devils themselves didn't like Sirko because he killed one of them in a pistol duel, resulting in the creation of the Chortomlyk River.

Voyage of Sirko to France. According to some sources, Ivan Sirko's army managed to bring "order" not only to Ukraine but also to France during the 30 Years' War. In just a few days, the men in trousers were able to accomplish what the French had struggled with for years – they conquered the impregnable fortress of Dunkirk. When the Cossacks came to collect payment for their services, the whimsical Cardinal Mazarin declared that the French, supposedly, fought for honor and glory, while the Cossacks fought for money. To this, he received a scornful reply that everyone fights for what they lack.

Among all the Cossacks, there was a jester whom his comrades loved for his simplicity. They say he might have been the only hetman who lived together with the Cossacks in the same barracks, sharing meals from the same pot and kindling the fire in the evenings. In addition to that, he was a daredevil and adventurer, always seeking new exploits, which endeared him even more to the soldiers.

"He fought in nearly 55 battles and never lost a single one. If for Ukrainians Sirko was the first legend in the village, then the Turks and Tatars hated him fiercely. Perhaps that's why they spread rumors that Sirko had some kind of magic, all the while nervously looking around, as who knows these characters..."

The legend of the letter from the Cossacks to the Turkish Sultan is associated with Ivan Sirko, who is credited with authorship of a letter sent to Sultan Mehmed IV. In the letter, it is said that Sirko made it clear to the Sultan that he is not just any treasure.

According to legend, the letter was written in 1676 by the Cossack hetman Ivan Sirko "with all the Cossacks of Zaporizhia" in response to an ultimatum from Sultan Mehmed (Muhammad) IV of the Ottoman Empire. The original letter did not survive, but in the 1870s, a copy made in the 18th century was discovered by the amateur ethnographer Y. P. Novitsky in Katerynoslav (now Dnipro, Ukraine). Novitsky passed it on to the renowned historian D. I. Yavornytsky, who once read it as a curiosity to his guests, including the artist I. Y. Repin. Repin became interested in the story and began a series of studies in 1880.

The Cossacks responded to his threatening letter with a mocking and defiant letter, filled with humor and insults. The Cossacks' response begins with a similar grandiose introduction, mocking the Sultan's titles and claiming extravagant titles for themselves. The tone is humorous and irreverent, and it is considered a classic example of Cossack wit and audacity.

The full response is quite lengthy, but here is a condensed version: "Sultan Mehmed IV, Emperor of the Ottomans, son of Ibrahim, brother of the Sun and Moon, grandson and regent of God on Earth, ruler of the kingdoms of Macedonia, Babylon, Jerusalem, Great and Little Egypt, king of kings, lord of lords, invincible knight, unmatched warrior, possessor of the Tree of Life, relentless guardian of the tomb of Jesus Christ, caretaker chosen by God, hope and comfort of Muslims, formidable and great defender of Christians, I command you, Zaporozhian Cossacks, to surrender to me voluntarily and without resistance, and do not force me to worry about your attacks."

The Cossacks' reply is a masterpiece of satire and remains a well-known example of the Cossack spirit in Ukrainian folklore.

The Christmas Battle at Sich. Sultan Mehmed IV, offended by the vulgar content of a cunningly devised letter, took offense and, at the first opportunity, marched on Sich with a massive army, calculating that the Cossacks would be drunk on Christmas Eve and peacefully sleeping. This turned out to be a fatal mistake. They managed to enter Sich, capturing the guards, but things took an unexpected turn from there. According to legend, one of the Cossacks woke up to the wind. Seeing through the window that the entire Sich was stuffed with Tatars like cockroaches, he immediately roused his comrades. The Cossacks, denied the luxury of finishing their dreams, were furious. Therefore, they warmly welcomed the Turks with bullets. The enemies, who did not expect such a reception, began to panic, knocking each other over. The Cossack marksmen skillfully mowed down the unwelcome guests, rapidly reducing their numbers. Realizing that a real beating was about to happen, the Sultan made the wisest decision in this situation – to beat a hasty retreat.

The right hand that brings victory. It is said that after his death, Sirko himself commanded to cut off his right hand and retrieve it in difficult moments. Why specifically the right hand and not, for example, the left, is not explained. Therefore, this moment is also considered a legend. Although there is a certain logic to it, who knows what to expect from people who carry a severed hand as an artifact?

The Ukrainian flag on the grave of Sirko. Few people know that one of the first Ukrainian flags was raised precisely at this sacred place on November 7, 1988. The residents of Pokrov (then Ordzhonikidze) raised the first blue and yellow flag. At that time, it was quite dangerous, especially considering that November 7 was celebrated as the Day of the October Revolution, and such an event did not meet approval from the local authorities.

Reburial of Ivan Sirko. Sirko knew no peace in life, and the same was true after his death. The first grave of the hetman was destroyed during the devastation of the Chortomlytska Sich. Later, he was reburied in the Kapulivka area, where locals took care of the grave. In 1939, Ivan Sirko was labeled a "Petlurist" and an "enemy of Soviet power." Therefore, no one cared for the grave of the unreliable "comrade" Sirko. In 1967, the grave was moved to its current location, during which the skull and several bones were extracted for research. Parts of the Cossack's remains traveled extensively—first to Moscow, where scientists, after studying the skull, could learn how the hetman looked. Then to Nikopol, and finally to Dnipro. People whispered that "it must be something with dark motives." It is even said that for several years, the skull was kept in the safe of some official. But finally, in 2000, the skull was returned to the body, and the ashes of the hetman were laid to rest.

Petro Kalnyshevsky

Petro Kalnyshevsky. The last hetman (military leader) of the Zaporizhian Cossacks

Petro Kalnyshevsky became the hetman (military leader) of the Zaporizhian Cossacks around 1765, at the age of 75. The Zaporizhian Cossacks were a semi-nomadic warrior group in the southern part of the Russian Empire. Russian Empress Catherine II: Empress Catherine II of Russia, also known as Catherine the Great, awarded Petro Kalnyshevsky.

In 1773, he was awarded the military rank of "Major General" in the Russian army. Upon entering the town of Romny, a majestic monument on Pokrovsky Hill comes into view. This monument celebrates the last hetman (chief) of the Zaporozhian Cossacks, Petro Kalnyshevsky. It was erected by the countrymen of the hetman in the summer of 1990, in preparation for the 300th anniversary of the "Cossack father's" birth. The monument is placed at the site where the Pokrovska Church stood until 1908, which was built with funds from Petro Kalnyshevsky and consecrated in 1770.

Due to his rebellious Cossack nature and love for Ukraine, Koshovyi was sent to the Solovetsky Monastery for life, where he was immured in a stone casemate without windows or doors, spending 12 years literally without seeing the light of day. Later, when he was almost 100 years old, he was transferred to a neighboring casemate, where the conditions were only slightly better, allowing occasional visits to the church under guard. Talking to Kalnyshevsky was strictly forbidden under the threat of severe punishment.

He was liberated at the age of 111, after Alexander I came to power in 1801. Kalnyshevsky passed away in the monastery in November 1803, at the age of 113. It is important to emphasize that he died without repentance, feeling spiritual righteousness.

For his entire life in the Sich, Petro Kalnyshevsky became a wealthy landowner. Upon his arrest at his winter quarters and hamlets, 639 horses, 1076 head of cattle, 14045 sheep, and 2175 puds of grain were listed. In the Romny Local Lore Museum, there is a precious Gospel that Petro Kalnyshevsky presented to the church of his native village Pustoviitivka. The entire world knows about this gift from the last hetman of the Zaporozhian Sich. Engraved on the bottom of the front cover is the inscription: "This Gospel book was made at the expense of the Zaporozhian Army's Lower Court Judge Military Petro Ivanovych Kalnyshevsky.

Chapter Seven
Currency Hryvnia

Hryvnia

In the time of Kievan Rus (IX–X centuries), the main currency on the territories of modern Ukraine was the Arab dirham, a silver coin that later equated to the Kievan hryvnia. This monetary system became widespread in Europe due to the intensive trade with Muslim countries. The first attempt to establish a local currency system was the minting conducted under the guidance of Prince Volodymyr the Great (963–1015) by Kievan goldsmiths and silversmiths. Many examples of these princely coins are known today.

The "Zlatnyk of Volodymyr" (Zlatnyk meaning "golden" in Ukrainian) had a weight of 4.4 grams, while the "Sribnyak" (a silver coin) had a variable weight ranging from 1.73 to 4.68 grams. These coins typically featured an image of the prince on the obverse (front side) and the princely family emblem, a trident, on the reverse side.

The obverse side usually displayed the likeness of the prince, with Volodymyr the Great being a prominent figure. Other princes who minted similar coins included his son Yaroslav the Wise (1019–1054), his second cousin Yaroslav Sviatoslav of Turov, and an unidentified Russian prince named Petro.

For instance, Yaroslav's silver coin featured the image of Saint George, the patron saint of princes, on the obverse side, and on the reverse side, the trident emblem was again present.

On the obverse (front) side, they usually engraved the image of the prince, while on the reverse (back) side, they depicted the princely family symbol – the trident. The hryvnia is mentioned in the "Primary Chronicle" by Nestor the Chronicler, where Prince Oleg imposed a tribute of 300 hryvnias per year on the Varangians. This reference dates back to the 9th century, providing evidence that the Ukrainian hryvnia is one of the oldest currencies in the world, with a history of at least 1200 years.

The Ukrainian hryvnia also played a role in the origin of the national currency of its northern neighbor. The word "ruble" was used by the inhabitants of Kievan Rus as early as the 12th century. However, it did not refer to money but rather to a piece, a chunk, or a wedge. During the Mongol-Tatar invasion, silver hryvnias were cut in half, giving rise to rubles – parts or chunks of the hryvnia.

It's important to note that the historical context of the word "ruble" in Kievan Rus had no direct connection to money; it simply denoted a portion or fragment, serving as a linguistic precursor to the later use of the term for currency.

The hryvnia was the main monetary unit in Rus' until the 14th century. It reappeared during moments of independence, initially in 1918 when the Ukrainian People's Republic (UNR) declared itself an "independent state, not dependent on anyone" through the Fourth Universal and symbolically reintroduced the hryvnia, which had been forgotten for centuries. The original symbol quickly became memorable to Ukrainian patriots.

On each banknote, it was stated that one hryvnia was equivalent to almost 9 (8.7) grams of pure gold. Ukraine did not have its own mint, so the banknotes were printed in Berlin. When the country gained independence, there was a need to issue a significant amount of money, and they turned to a Canadian company for assistance. However, this company couldn't produce the required 1.5 billion banknotes, so English involvement was also sought.

Originally, there were plans to release banknotes with denominations of 3 and 25 hryvnias, but they were later replaced with 2 and 20 hryvnias. Additionally, the issuance of 3, 15, and 20 kopecks was abandoned. The official introduction of the hryvnia into circulation took place on August 25, 1996, with an exchange rate of 100,000 karbovanets for 1 hryvnia.

Chapter Eight

A decree for the liquidation of the Zaporizhian Sich.

How Russian Empire tried to destroy the spirit of freedom of Cossacks.

On August 14, 1775, Empress Catherine II issued a decree for the liquidation of the Zaporozhian Sich. The manifesto had a loud title, "On the Destruction of the Zaporozhian Sich," and began as follows: "We have desired through this to declare to all Our Empire for general knowledge that the Zaporozhian Sich is completely destroyed, with the extermination for the future of even the name of the Zaporozhian Cossacks, no less than an offense to Our Imperial Majesty."

"Ukrainian identity and the Cossack spirit were gladly eradicated by fire and sword"

Three months before the issuance of the Manifesto on the Elimination of the Zaporozhian Sich on May 14, the Empress brought another calamity to Ukraine - serfdom, which contradicted the very spirit of the Cossacks.

The queen "rewarded" the Cossacks for their contribution in the Russo-Turkish War of 1768-1774. During this conflict, the Zaporizhian Cossacks provided significant military support by mobilizing 7,500 cavalry and 5,800 infantry, as well as equipping a fleet of Cossack boats. The Cossacks had extensive experience in warfare against the Turks, participating in battles such as Ochakov, storming Perekop, capturing Kaffa, undertaking campaigns to Izmail, and playing a crucial role in the battles at Larz and Kagul.

After the war, the Cossacks returned to their native Zaporizhian Sich. However, the majority of them dispersed to relatives, friends, and families to spend the winter and rest from the war. Only a few thousand soldiers remained on the Sich itself. Seizing the opportunity in May 1775, a corps led by General Petro Tekeli was sent to the stronghold of Cossack freedom. This corps consisted of 10 infantry and 13 Don Cossack regiments, 8 regiments of regular cavalry, 20 hussar squadrons, and 17 pioneer squadrons.

Meanwhile, on the Sich, the Cossacks convened a council led by the host hetman Petro Kalnyshevsky. Fearing the bloody revenge of the Russians on their families in case of resistance, the warriors decided to lay down their weapons. Ukrainians vividly remembered the year 1709 – Peter I's punitive expedition and the massacre in Baturyn. Despite the inevitable death in battle, a significant number of Cossacks were unwilling to surrender to Catherine. However, others resolved, "We have parents and children; the Muscovite will cut them down!"

The active participation in the destruction of the Zaporizhian Sich was taken by the Don Cossacks. Although they, despite their loyalty to the tsarina, received "gratitude" in the early 1790s. They incurred the anger of St. Petersburg, lost part of the previously gifted lands, and were resettled to remote regions of the empire.

The Treaty of Pereyaslav, also known as the Pereyaslav Articles, was indeed signed on March 31, 1654, and it marked an important historical event for Ukraine. The agreement involved the acceptance of the Zaporozhian Cossacks under the overlordship of the Russian Tsar Alexei Mikhailovich. Ukrainian envoys prepared the text, and the Moscow side only approved 11 articles with minor amendments.

The negotiations were initiated by the Ukrainians themselves, and Orest Subtelny, in his renowned book "Ukraine: A History," emphasizes a key circumstance that prompted the Cossacks to seek the protection of the Tsar. In January 1654, at the Pereyaslav Council, the hetman (not a prince), representing a de facto liberated country, emphasized the necessity of a supreme ruler. During those times, sovereignty was associated not with the people but with the person of the legitimate (recognized) monarch. Given the medieval antagonism with Catholics and "Turks" (Muslims), the ancestors chose an Orthodox tsar.

It's important to note that this historical event occurred in a complex geopolitical context, and the decision to align with Russia was influenced by various factors, including the desire for protection against external threats and the political realities of the time.

At the time when the "brotherhood" in the Russo-Turkish War was devastating Ukrainians, their former enemy, the Turkish Sultan Mustafa III, allocated lands beyond the Danube to the Cossacks who had escaped from Russian terror. He also bestowed regalia, including a mace, nunchaku, seal, and a banner consecrated by the Patriarch of Constantinople. This was a gesture indicating that he had no objections to the Orthodox faith of the Cossacks. Ataman Kalnyshevsky, the last Ataman of Zaporizhian Sich, who was sentenced to life imprisonment on the Solovetsky Islands by the order of Catherine II. He spent the next 25 years of his life in solitary confinement, unable to communicate with anyone, not even the monks of the Solovetsky monastery. Once a year, on Easter, the Ataman was allowed to go outside. The Empress regularly inquired about the last Koshovyi Ataman of the Zaporizhian Sich, wondering if he was still alive and if he had any intentions of repentance. She expressed surprise that the Ataman managed to survive for such a long time.

Only in 1801 did Emperor Alexander I grant forgiveness to Kalnyshevsky and allow him to return to Ukraine. However,

Kalnyshevsky chose to embrace monasticism and remained in the monastery, where he passed away in 1803. At the time of his death, he was 113 years old. In 2008, the Ukrainian Church canonized Petro Kalnyshevsky as a saint and martyr. It is appropriate to commemorate him along with all Ukrainian heroes on October 14, during the celebration of the Intercession of the Theotokos.

In 2008, the Ukrainian Church canonized Petro Kalnyshevsky as a holy venerable martyr. It is customary to commemorate him along with all Ukrainian heroes on October 14th, during the Feast of the Protection of the Mother of God (Pokrov). However, there is a tradition of commemorating saints on the anniversary of their death.

According to accounts from Cossacks, after the defeat of the Zaporozhian Sich, when the church of St. Pokrov was burning, Kalnyshevsky reportedly said, "I am no more; I died together with the Cossack liberty!" And indeed, the Cossack liberty perished according to the decree of Empress Catherine II on this very day – August 14, 1775, in the region of Makiyivka.

"After the liquidation of the Zaporozhian Cossacks, they were resettled, but they did not take their treasures with them, as they were confident that they would return soon. The Cossacks scattered to different corners of the country, passing away, growing old, yet the legends of the treasures and signs of their discovery were passed down from mouth to mouth to grandchildren and great-grandchildren. Centuries have passed since the times of glorious campaigns and the turbulent life of the Zaporozhian Host, and still, researchers and treasure hunters continue to seek riches along the Dnieper. Perhaps, you too will find something?"

Ukrainian Cossacks were renowned as excellent infantrymen in Europe, boasting a formidable fleet and intriguing traditions. Legends and books abound about the distinctive character of the Cossacks, and their military exploits continue to inspire modern Ukrainian warriors. As long as the memory of our ancestors is not forgotten, Cossack heritage thrives in tales, legends, books, and historical legacy, providing us with a rich source of inspiration!

Cossack treasure

One famous legend speaks of a particularly valuable treasure hidden by a renowned Cossack leader. It is said that he chose a deserted island in the middle of the Dnieper as the burial site for his immense wealth. To keep the location a secret, he devised a complex map that only a select few knew how to decipher.

Over time, as the Cossack brotherhood faced external threats and internal conflicts, some of these treasures were lost or forgotten. Many stories claim that the Dnieper River itself became a repository for the riches of the Cossacks, hiding countless treasures beneath its depths.

To this day, there are tales of fortune hunters and adventurers seeking the legendary Cossack treasures, diving into the waters of the Dnieper or exploring the remote islands in the hope of uncovering the long-buried wealth of the Zaporozhian Cossacks. Whether these treasures are real or exist only in the realm of myth and legend, they continue to capture the imagination and curiosity of those drawn to the rich history of the Cossack warriors.

In the times of campaigns and victorious battles in the Zaporozhian Sich, a considerable amount of treasures, gold, and trophies accumulated in the free Cossack territory. Every Cossack was obliged to have his own treasure after campaigns and kept it in a securely hidden place. There was also a separate treasury for the Zaporozhian army as a whole. After a campaign, the Cossacks would gather, divide the spoils, and then hide them in the Dnieper River.

Legends tell of the cunning and secretive ways in which the Cossacks concealed their treasures. They would choose remote and inaccessible locations along the Dnieper, such as small islands or hidden riverbanks, to bury their wealth. The treasure locations were carefully guarded secrets passed down through generations or shared only among the most trusted comrades.

Today, we can take pride in the absence of homegrown autocrats. On the other hand, recognizing our own (not foreign!) monarchy of that period as a historically necessary link in the societal evolution towards the presently internally organized national states of Europe is appropriate. Agreeably, even in the majority of Russians, there is a distorted but their own "core," while we, on the contrary, still unsuccessfully "sort out" ourselves, as if cursed.

On this day, the Hotin Battle concluded, marking the 400th anniversary of a significant civilization victory. On September 29, 1621, negotiations began between the Polish-Cossack command and the Ottoman-Tatar forces, eventually leading to the signing of a peace agreement on October 8, 1621. Zaporozhian Cossacks, led by Hetman Petro Sahaidachny, played a decisive role in defeating the army of Ottoman Sultan Osman II near Hotin. As a result of this victory, the Asian empire abandoned its plans for the conquest of Europe.

Chapter Nine
A little about historical geography.

Many ancient societies, including those in what is now Ukraine, had advanced agricultural practices, sophisticated social structures, and intricate belief systems. The perception of these cultures as "wild" or "primitive" often stems from a Eurocentric view that places Western civilizations on a pedestal.

The division of the world into Europe and Asia is purely conventional. It is considered that they form a single continent. In ancient times, the division between Europe and Asia (more accurately, Asia) was not based on geographical features but rather on socio-cultural distinctions. The boundaries between them were purely arbitrary.

In ancient times, the most common border was along the Tanais River. At that time, it was the present-day Siverskyi Donets, and the present-day Don was considered its tributary. The Siverskyi Donets originates from the Central Russian Upland. It is important to note that in Russian history, the name "Siverskyi Donets" is as relevant as a guinea pig to the sea.

In the vicinity of the Tanais (Don) River, Alexander the Great sought the Land of the Gods (as the word "Asia" is translated). It was once said: Europe is the land of humans; Asia is the land of gods. According to apocrypha, it is here that the beloved disciple of Christ, the apostle John, embarked on a mission to "seek the bright race" – clearly, whose.

...They began to establish a hypothetical border along the Ural Mountains between Europe and Asia at the insistence of Peter I. He was eager to consider himself European, even though the lands of Muscovy did not belong to either Europe or Asia. On old maps, these lands were marked as Tartary. This name does not come from the Tatars; on the contrary, a part of the Turkic people received this name due to Tartary, which originates from the ancient Greek Tartarus.

European geographers do not care at all about where some Tsar Tartary draws the border. For them, I repeat, it is one continent. Moscow's money decided everything then, as it does now. For example, the illiterate lover of Peter, the "semi-sovereign ruler" Menshikov, simply bought himself the title of a member of the Royal Society in London (one of the oldest and most respected scientific organizations in the world), where such trivialities as a border that nobody needs are of no concern.

This could be talked about a lot more, including the fact that Kyiv, referred to as Azagorium or Metropolis (the capital) was already marked on Ptolemy's map, indicating its existence in the 1st century with its own church at that time. However, even without this, a long read has emerged – not everyone has the patience to finish such a tedious and complex text.

Geographical center of Europe

Geographical center of Europe, Ukraine

There are several variations as to where the center of Europe is located. In 1885-1887, geographers from the Imperial Royal Military Geographical Institute in Vienna determined that the geographic center of Europe is in the village of Dilove, Zakarpattia region. They conducted geodetic research in the territory of the present-day Zakarpattia region.

Asia and Europe division

The division of Europe and Asia being considered one continent is based on tectonic plates and landmass continuity. The traditional division between Europe and Asia, often along the Ural Mountains and the Ural River, has been used for centuries. However, as you noted, in ancient times, the division between these regions was more fluid and based on cultural and social factors.

The idea that our ancestors were "wild pagans" is a common stereotype that doesn't accurately reflect the complexity and sophistication of ancient cultures. Many ancient civilizations had advanced systems of governance, art, science, and philosophy. It's important to approach the study of history with an open mind and avoid overly simplistic interpretations.

The historical boundary along the Tanais (Don) River is indeed a fascinating example. In ancient times, this river served as a cultural and political boundary between different groups of people. The fluidity of such borders reflects the dynamic nature of human societies and how they interacted with their environment.

Then it was the present-day Siversky Donets, and the present-day Don was considered its tributary. The Siversky Donets originates from the Central Russian Upland. I want to emphasize: for Russia, this name has as much relevance as a guinea pig to the sea.

There is an opinion that the Rus people are not Vikings but rather originated from the Ukrainian Steppe, specifically the Siversky

Donets-Don-North Caucasus region. It associates them with the Roxolani, also known as the "light Alans," and suggests a connection to ancient Iranian peoples, referring to them as the "light Aryans."

It's important to note that the origins of the Rus people are a topic of historical debate, and there are different theories about their roots. The traditional view connects the Rus people with the Varangians and Vikings, who played a significant role in the early history of the East Slavic region, including the formation of the Kievan Rus.

The idea that the Rus have roots in the Ukrainian Steppe and are connected to the Roxolani or Alans is one of the alternative theories that have been proposed by some historians.

Luhansk

Luhansk did not appear in an empty place - various peoples have long lived here."

In ancient times, these lands belonged to Turkic-speaking nomads and were part of the vast Polovtsian Field or Kipchak Steppe during the era of the Kyivan Rus. Later, they became known as the Wild Fields – these were perilous territories, yet they were never uninhabited.

Certainly, the first known permanent settlements in the territory of modern Luhansk have names of Ukrainian origin, such as Vergunka (named after the wintering place of the Cossack Semen Vergun), the estate of Veselenka, Kam'yanyy Brid, and Krasnyy Yar (yes, "krasnyy" is also a Ukrainian word and not a Surzhyk term; it is a rarely used synonym for "beautiful" or "splendid").

In the 18th century, these settlements became part of the Kalmyk palanka of the Zaporozhian Sich. They were quite sizable communities with their own churches. For example, in Kam'yanyy Brod, the Petro-Pavlivska Church was consecrated in 1761. According to reports from Muscovite officials, it was noted that a "Little Russian people" had long been living there.

The second half of the 18th century witnessed the final subjugation of the Ukrainian Cossack state by the Russian Empire. The remnants of autonomy were eliminated, the Sich (Cossack stronghold) was destroyed, the Ukrainian elite was Russified, and the local population was transformed into serfs. Free Cossacks in the Lugansk region became known as "military settlers."

During the same period, the Muscovites are conducting a social experiment and creating Slavyano-Serbia in this region. It also began as military settlements, with a hussar regiment formed on the lands of Ukrainian Cossacks, composed of people from the Balkans and contemporary Moldova.

New administrative units called "shants" or "rots were established." For example, the Vergunsky shant is also referred to as the Second Rota. Later, the Lugansk Pioneer Regiment was stationed here, with the "pioneers" being former Ukrainian Cossacks, and they were led by the future hero of the 1812 war, Mikhail Kutuzov.

In 1795, on the banks of the River Luhan in the area of present-day Luhansk, construction of an iron foundry (actually, a cannon foundry) began under the order of Empress Catherine the Great. Most modern historians mistakenly consider the date of the empress's order as the founding moment of Luhansk. And, of course, they are mistaken.

One more detail: the construction of the factory only began in the following year, and the settlement will emerge only three years later. Until then, the builders lived in Kam'yanyi Brod and Verguntsi. Oh, and one very small detail: in the queen's decree, there is no mention of founding a city, only a factory. Yes, there will be a workers' settlement functioning alongside the factory, which will be called Luhansk Zavod (Luhansk Factory), but it is not a city at all.

The true founding date of Luhansk is September 3, 1882, when by the order of the great-grandson of Catherine II, Tsar Alexander III, the settlements on either side of the Luhanka River – Kamianyi Brid and Luhansk Livarnyi Zavod – were merged into a single town. The newly formed town, inhabited by over 10,000 people, became the new center of the Slovianoserbsk County in the Katerynoslav Governorate.

Crimea

The history of Crimea is rich in events and the interweaving of various cultural influences, as this region is situated at the crossroads of paths and interactions of different civilizations. Renowned for its natural beauty, diverse history, and rich cultural heritage, Crimea has been the site of many significant events and legends.

Scythians and Taurians: In ancient times, Crimea was home to Scythian and Taurian tribes. Their culture and empire left traces in archaeology and legends.

Greek Era: In the 6th century BCE, Greeks established colonies on the southern coast, such as Chersonesus Taurica. This period marked the influence of Greek culture and interaction with local populations.

Roman Empire: Crimea came under the rule of the Roman Empire, contributing to the region's development.

Medieval Period: During the Middle Ages, Crimea became an emirate under the influence of the caliphate. Later, the Crimean Khanate emerged and existed until the mid-19th century.

Ottoman Empire: In 1475, Crimea fell under the control of the Ottoman Empire and remained part of it until the mid-19th century.

Russian Empire and Soviet Union: Following the Russo-Turkish War in the mid-19th century, Crimea became part of the Russian Empire. Later, the Crimean Khanate was annexed by the Soviet Union in 1944 during World War II.

Contemporary Period: After the dissolution of the Soviet Union, Crimea became part of independent Ukraine. However, in 2014, following a controversial referendum, Russia annexed Crimea.

Chapter Ten
Some interesting historical facts

Kyivan Rus' (980-1054)

Kyiv was founded in 482 AD, and the mass baptism of the Kyivans took place in 988 AD, initiated by Grand Prince Volodymyr (Vladimir) of Kyiv (956-1015). Moscow, on the other hand, was traditionally considered to be founded in 1147 by Yuri Dolgorukiy. However, it's worth noting that Yuri Dolgorukiy did not establish Moscow himself but rather seized it from a Suzdal boyar named

Kuchka Stepán Ivánovich, who owned villages along the Moscow River. Dolgorukiy accomplished this by killing Kuchka.

Yuri Dolgoruky was indeed a descendant of Vladimir Svyatoslavich, who played a key role in the Christianization of Kievan Rus. Yuri Dolgoruky was the founder of Moscow and the Grand Prince of Suzdal and Kiev. However, there is a historical inaccuracy in the statement about Yuri Dolgoruky's burial.

Yuri Dolgoruky is not buried near the Kiev Pechersk Lavra. Instead, he is traditionally believed to be buried in the Saviour Monastery of St. Euthymius (Spaso-Yevfimiev Monastery) in Suzdal, Russia. This monastery, located in the Vladimir Region, was founded by Yuri Dolgoruky in the 12th century. It became the burial place for Yuri Dolgoruky and several other rulers of Suzdal.

The Kiev Pechersk Lavra, on the other hand, is associated with the burials of many prominent figures in Kievan Rus, including saints and princes, but Yuri Dolgoruky is not among them.

For our northern neighbors as well, Kyiv is a sacred place! The territory of Kyivan Rus was as follows: - In the 11th century: 800,000 square kilometers - In the 12th century: 1,300,000 square kilometers.

The statement "Kyivan Rus extended from the Black Sea to the Baltic and White Seas" is a common historical assertion. Kyivan Rus was a medieval East Slavic state that existed from the late 9th to the mid-13th century, and it covered a vast territory that included parts of modern-day Ukraine, Belarus, and Russia.

First time the name "Ukraine" was mentioned in the Kyiv Chronicle in 1187. The term "Ukraine" itself has its roots in the Old East Slavic word "krajina". And has no relation to 'periphery' whatsoever; on the contrary, the root of the word 'Krai' (Країна) is 'state.'

The name 'Russian Empire' was coined by Peter I, who renamed the Moscow State on October 22, 1721, using the name of another state. In those times, Rus' was already a prestigious and respected European brand. The Kyivan princes-maintained family ties with practically all royal houses in Europe. I remember the chapel of St. Margaret in Edinburgh, where it is stated that she is the granddaughter of Kyivan Prince Yaroslav the Wise (!).

Rus' was one of the European centers of education. The first educational institution is mentioned in the year 988 in the Tale of Bygone Years. The second one appeared in 1030, created by Yaroslav the Wise in Novgorod. The Ostroh Academy was founded in 1576, and the Kyiv-Mohyla Academy in 1615. The Kyiv-Mohyla Academy itself became the cradle of Russian education. Graduates of the academy were the founders of a number of schools in Russia and Belarus, especially in the 18th century.

Schools and seminaries were established in almost every city in Russia, including Moscow, St. Petersburg, Smolensk, Rostov, Tobolsk, Irkutsk, Kholmogory, Tver, Belgorod, Suzdal, Vyatka, Vologda, Kolomna, Ryazan, Pskov, Veliky Ustyug, Astrakhan, Kostroma, Vladimir on the Klyazma, and other cities. The teachers in these schools were predominantly graduates of the Kiev Academy.

The renowned scientist Mikhail Lomonosov was also a graduate of the Kyiv-Mohyla Academy. However, prior to that, he completed the "Spasskaya School," founded by an alumnus of the same Kyiv-Mohyla Academy.

It is also important to remember Ukrainian soldiers. Throughout Europe, not just from textbooks, people know about Ukrainian Cossacks. In almost all European wars, of which there were hundreds, every third mercenary was a Ukrainian Cossack. The history of World War II would not be the same without Ukrainians. Terrifying statistics speak to this, as over 50% of the Soviet Union's casualties were Ukrainians. It is extremely uncomfortable for Russia to be a global actor without its own history, name, and people. After all, "Russian" is not a nationality, but rather an affiliation with a territory.

Some comparison of Russia and Ukraine history

Russia: The Russian Academy of Sciences was founded in 1724, and Moscow University was established in 1755.

Ukraine: The Ostroh Academy was founded in 1576, and Lviv University was established in 1661.

The printed primer (Alphabet Book) in Ukraine emerged in 1574 in Lviv, while in the Muscovy Tsardom, it happened 60 years later, in 1634.

The Kyivan Metropolis was established in 988, while the Moscow Metropolis was founded only in 1458. The Kyivan Metropolis is 460 years older than the Moscow Metropolis.

The capitals: Kyiv was founded in the year 482, while the city of Moscow was founded in 1147 by Yuri Dolgoruky, the son of Vladimir Monomakh. Kyiv is older than Moscow by 665 years.

The first monarch crowned in the Muscovite Tsardom was Ivan the Terrible in the year 1547. In the lands of ancient Ukraine, it was Danylo Halytsky in the year 1253.

Kyiv got rid of the Mongol yoke in 1363 after the Battle of the Blue Waters, Moscow shook off the yoke in 1480 after the Stand on the Ugra River, and tribute to the Crimean Khanate was paid until the year 1700, including the early years of Peter the Great's reign.

Chapter Eleven

Many linguists think that the Russian language is artificial.

The Russian language is a blend of several languages and dialects, essentially an Esperanto of Old Bulgarian (ecclesiastical), Turkic, Finno-Ugric, Ruthenian (Ukrainian), Greek, Polish, German, and Latin words. It features a semi-Finnish grammar rather than a Slavic one.

All this mixture ultimately became the basis for the current Russian language, coinciding lexically only by 30-40% with other Slavic languages, where (including Belarusian and Ukrainian) this coincidence is incomparably higher, reaching 70-80%. Therefore, from a linguistic perspective, the Russian language should be referred to not as "East Slavic" but as a Finno-Slavic language.

The Russians themselves are Slavicized Finns (!).

The territories inhabited by ancient pre-Slavic ethnic groups include only Smolensk, Kursk, Bryansk – the territories of the ancient Krivichs (Slavicized by Western Slavs of the Balts). The remaining lands are Finnish, where no Slavs ever lived: Chud, Merya, Mordva, Perm, Vyatichi, and others (!).

A.A. Shakhmatov and other Russian linguists discussed the idea that the Russian language was artificially created and is essentially a

Moscow dialect in Shakhmatov's book "An Outline of the Contemporary Russian Literary Language" (Uchpedgiz, 1941).

The Russian language is a Church Slavonic language and, by its origin, is a Bulgarian language that over centuries has converged with the living Finno-Ugric language of the people.

Peter the Great borrowed the name "Russia" from "Kievan Rus", whose rulers had familial ties with various royal houses in Europe.

Kyivan Rus has nothing in common with Russia because historically, Kyivan Rus predates Muscovy by a significant margin. (Kyivan Rus – 9th century, Moscovy – 13 th century)

The large Moscow state was multiethnic and consequently multilingual. That is why there was a necessity to have a unified state language, which was established and formalized by the decree of the tsar.

Russia officially became known as "Russia" for the first time under Peter the Great, who considered the previous name, "Muscovy," to be "dark and superstitious."

Peter not only forcibly shaved beards, prohibited women in Muscovy from wearing chadors in the Asian manner (!), and banned harems (a place where women were kept in confinement), but also, during his travels in Europe, pressured cartographers to label his country not as Muscovy or Muscovitia as before, but as "Russia." He also aimed to have Muscovites themselves recognized as Slavs for the first time in history, which was part of the overall strategy of "opening a window to Europe."

Chapter Twelve

Ukrainian language is the language of the nightingale!

The Ukrainian language was recognized as the most beautiful, melodic, and rich language in the world at the language beauty contest in Paris in 1934, taking second place after Italian.

In 2012, she was included in the Guinness World Records book, securing the top spot for the longest duration of a national song musical telethon, and has held the record ever since.

"Only Ukrainian compositions were played continuously without interruption for 110 hours in a live broadcast. The previous record was set by Italy in 2010 in the city of Pesaro, lasting 103 hours, 9 minutes, and 26 seconds."

Ukrainians are a singing nation that has created the largest number of folk songs in the world. Approximately 200,000 Ukrainian folk songs have been counted. No other nation in history has produced such a quantity of songs independently as the Ukrainian people.

In UNESCO, there is a remarkable sound archive of folk songs from around the world. Ukraine's collection alone comprises 15,500 songs.

Over the past 400 years, there have been several attempts to restrict the use of the Ukrainian language. It can be characterized as linguistic oppression or attempts at linguistic assimilation.

1622 — The decree of Tsar Mikhail, based on the submission of Moscow Patriarch Filaret, to burn all copies of the printed "Evangelical Teacher" by K. Stavrovetsky in the state of Moscow.

1696 — Resolution of the Polish Sejm on the introduction of the Polish language in courts and institutions of Right-Bank Ukraine.

1690 — Condemnation and anathema by the Synod of the Russian Orthodox Church on the "Kiev new books" of P. Mohyla, K. Stavrovetsky, S. Polotsky, L. Baranovych, A. Radziwill, and others.

1720 — Peter the Great's decree prohibiting the printing of books in the Ukrainian language and the removal of Ukrainian texts from church books.

1729 - Decree by Peter II to rewrite all state resolutions and orders from Ukrainian to Russian.

1763 - Catherine II's decree prohibiting the use of the Ukrainian language in the Kyiv-Mohyla Academy.

1769 - Synod of the Russian Orthodox Church's prohibition on printing and using Ukrainian primers.

1775 - Destruction of the Zaporizhian Sich and closure of Ukrainian schools associated with Cossack chancelleries.

1789 - Order from the Education Commission of the Polish Sejm to close all Ukrainian schools.

In 1817, the introduction of the Polish language in all public schools in Western Ukraine took place.

In 1832, the reorganization of education in Right-Bank Ukraine occurred on imperial principles, with a shift to Russian as the language of instruction.

In 1847, the Kirilo-Mefodiyevsky Society was defeated, leading to intensified persecution of the Ukrainian language and culture. The prohibition of the best works of Shevchenko, Kulish, Kostomarov, and others also occurred during this time.

In 1859, the Ministry of Religious Affairs and Education of Austria-Hungary attempted to the Ukrainian Cyrillic alphabet with the Latin alphabet in Eastern Galicia and replace Bukovina.

In 1862, free Ukrainian Sunday schools for adults were closed in the sub-Russian Ukraine.

In 1863, the Valuyev Circular was issued, prohibiting the issuance of censorship permits for the printing of Ukrainian spiritual and popular educational literature, claiming that "there was and could be no separate Little Russian language."

The Consul of Russia stated: Ukraine was invented by Austrians, and the Ukrainian language by the communists. In 1864, the Statute on Primary Education was adopted, stipulating that education should be conducted only in the Russian language.

In 1869, the Polish language was introduced as the official language of education and administration in Eastern Galicia.

In 1870, the Minister of Education of Russia, D. Tolstoy, explained that the "ultimate goal of the education of all non-Russians should unquestionably be Russification."

In 1876, Alexander's Ems Ukase prohibited the printing and importation of any Ukrainian-language literature from abroad, as well as the prohibition of Ukrainian stage performances and printing of Ukrainian texts under musical notation, i.e., folk songs.

In 1881, the teaching of Ukrainian language in public schools and the delivery of church sermons in Ukrainian were banned.

In 1884, Alexander III prohibited Ukrainian theatrical performances in all Little Russian gubernias. In 1888, Alexander III issued a decree banning the use of the Ukrainian language in official institutions and the christening of individuals with Ukrainian names.

1892 — Ban on translating books from Russian into Ukrainian.

1895 — Ban by the Main Administration for Printing Affairs on publishing Ukrainian books for children.

1911 — Resolution of the VII Noble Assembly in Moscow on exclusively Russian-language education and the inadmissibility of using other languages in Russian schools.

1914 — Ban on celebrating the 100th anniversary of Taras Shevchenko; Nicholas II's decree on the abolition of the Ukrainian press.

The term "Zhydo-Mazepintsy" refers to the opponents of the celebration of Taras Shevchenko's jubilee in 1914 and 1916, during the campaigns of Russification in Western Ukraine.

The Black Hundreds, as they were known, advocated for the prohibition of the Ukrainian language, education, and the Ukrainian Church.

In 1922, part of the leadership of the Central Committee of the Russian Communist Party (Bolsheviks) and the Central Committee of the Communist Party (Bolsheviks) of Ukraine declared the "theory" of the struggle in Ukraine between two cultures – urban (Russian) and rural (Ukrainian), with the former expected to triumph.

In 1924, the Polish Republic enacted a law restricting the use of the Ukrainian language in administrative bodies, the judiciary, and education in territories inhabited by Ukrainians. Additionally, in the same year, the Kingdom of Romania passed a law obliging all "Romanians" who "lost their mother tongue" to provide education to their children exclusively in Romanian schools.

1925 — the final closure of the Ukrainian "secret" university in Lviv.

1926 — Stalin's letter to Comrade Kaganovich and other members of the Politburo of the Central Committee of the Communist Party (Bolshevik) of Ukraine, sanctioning the struggle against "national deviation" and the beginning of the persecution of advocates of "Ukrainization."

1933 — Stalin's telegram on the cessation of "Ukrainization."

1933 — the annulment in Romania of the ministerial decree of December 31, 1929, which allowed a few hours of Ukrainian language instruction per week in schools with a majority of Ukrainian students.

1934 — a special order from the Ministry of Education of Romania regarding the dismissal from work, "for hostile attitude towards the state and the Romanian people," of all Ukrainian teachers demanding the return of Ukrainian language instruction in schools.

1938 — the resolution of the People's Commissariat of the USSR and the Central Committee of the All-Union Communist Party (Bolsheviks) "On the mandatory study of the Russian language in schools of national republics and regions," with a corresponding resolution from the People's Commissariat of the Ukrainian SSR and the Central Committee of the Communist Party (Bolshevik) of Ukraine.

In 1947, the "Vistula Operation" took place; the resettlement of a portion of Ukrainians from ethnic Ukrainian lands "scattered" among Poles in Western Poland to accelerate their Polonization.

The "Vistula Action" was the final act of the Polish-Ukrainian tragedy in 1958, which solidified in Article 20 of the Legislation of the USSR and allied republics on public education the provision for the free choice of the language of instruction. This allowed the study of all languages, except Russian, according to the parents' preferences for their children.

From 1960 to 1980, there was a mass closure of Ukrainian schools in Poland and Romania. In 1970, a directive was issued stating that dissertations could only be defended in the Russian language.

In 1972, party authorities prohibited the celebration of the anniversary of I. Kotliarevsky's museum in Poltava.

In 1973, there was a ban on celebrating the anniversary of I. Kotliarevsky's work "Eneida".

1974 – Resolution of the Central Committee of the Communist Party of the Soviet Union (CPSU) "On preparation for the 50th anniversary of the creation of the Union of Soviet Socialist Republics," where the creation of a "new historical community – the Soviet people" is proclaimed for the first time, officially endorsing a course towards denationalization.

1978 – Resolution of the Central Committee of the CPSU and the Council of Ministers of the Soviet Union "On measures for further improving the study and teaching of the Russian language in the union republics" (Brezhnev Circular).

1983 – Resolution of the Central Committee of the CPSU and the Council of Ministers of the Soviet Union "On additional measures to improve the study of the Russian language in general education

In the USSR, during the specified period:

1984: The Central Committee of the Communist Party of the Soviet Union (CPSU) and the Council of Ministers of the USSR issued a decree "On further improvement of general secondary education for youth and improvement of the working conditions of the general education school." The content of this decree is not specified.

1984: An increase of 15% in salary for teachers of the Russian language compared to teachers of the Ukrainian language began in the USSR.

1984: The Ministry of Culture of the USSR issued an order for the transfer of documentation in all museums of the Soviet Union to the Russian language.

1989: The Central Committee of the CPSU issued a decree on the "legislative consolidation of the Russian language as the state language." This indicated an official preference for the Russian language.

1990: The Supreme Soviet of the USSR adopted the Law on the Languages of the Peoples of the USSR, where the Russian language was granted the status of an official language.

In 2012, the Ukrainian Parliament adopted the draft law "On the Principles of State Language Policy," which posed a significant threat of narrowing the scope of the use of the Ukrainian language in key areas of life in most regions of Ukraine.

Chapter Thirteen
The Great Ukrainians

It is not a ranking but a list in which outstanding individuals are named according to the chronological order of their birth dates, in reverse order—from our prehistoric times.

Defenders of Azovstal.

For 82 days, several thousand Ukrainian soldiers - members of the Azov Regiment, Marines, border guards, territorial defense forces, as well as employees of the Security Service of Ukraine and the National Police - did what will undoubtedly be included in the textbooks of modern Ukrainian history: under relentless shelling and bombardment, surrounded, they repelled constant attacks from superior enemy forces in Mariupol.

Once a nearly half-million-strong industrial port city, this city was completely cut off from Ukraine in the early days of the full-scale war. However, its garrison stubbornly held back the enemy, slowly retreating to the last "fortress" - the Azovstal metallurgical plant. The battle for it lasted from April to mid-May. Ukrainian forces, despite a shortage of weapons, ammunition, medicines, and food, despite almost complete lack of communication with the "mainland," fought to the last. Many civilians and wounded, without access to basic medications, were with the fighters all the time. And the Russians deliberately bombed the underground facility that served as a hospital.

And still, the defenders did not surrender their weapons, turning to the leaders of major states, international organizations, and even to the Pope, appealing to organize their extraction to some third country. And they did not lose optimism.

On May 16, when all the strength was exhausted, the military command ordered Ukrainian fighters to preserve their lives and leave

Azovstal. Since then, approximately 2,500 of them, through the mediation of the UN and the International Committee of the Red Cross, ended up in Russian captivity.

The enemy, unforgiving, took courage from them - almost fifty 'Azov' fighters were killed by the occupiers in the Olenivka colony. The struggle to liberate the rest continues.

Volodymir Zelensky

(B orn: 1978) is the President of Ukraine and a political figure. He enjoys worldwide popularity. His addresses have been listened to – and applauded – by the parliaments of almost all democratic states on the planet and assemblies of representatives of the most influential international organizations. Top-tier media write about him. There is hardly another person in Ukraine with such a level of recognition globally.

After the onset of the major war, Zelensky, unexpectedly for many, demonstrated his ability to lead the country that came under attack by one of the most powerful armies in the world. Entrusting the military sphere to the Chief of the General Staff of the Armed Forces of Ukraine, Valeriy Zaluzhnyi, Zelensky focused— and does so extremely energetically— on the crucial task of ensuring broad international support for Ukraine—politically, militarily, and economically.

Before the sixth president, there will still be questions: about traitors in the government, about the rapid loss of the south and far from ideal preparation for war, about personnel policy, and more. But all of this will be after. For now, the war continues, and the country, along with Zelensky, is holding its ground. And even preparing to regain everything lost before.

Oleg Sentsov

Year of birth: 1976
Director, screenwriter

For five years, the global elite, from Hollywood stars to religious authorities, fought for the release of Oleg Sentsov, the most famous Russian political prisoner-Ukrainian.

He, an activist of AutoMaidan during the Revolution of Dignity, was arrested by Russian special services after the occupation of Crimea by the Russian Federation. Subsequently, a 'court' sentenced him to 20 years in a strict regime colony on fabricated charges of terrorism.

Sentsov only obtained his freedom as part of a prisoner exchange. After his release in September 2019, he spent about a year speaking about Ukraine on reputable global platforms. Subsequently, two full-length directorial works by Sencov were released – 'Numbers' (co-directed with Akhtem Seitablaiev) and 'Rhino.' Since the onset of the full-scale Russian invasion, he volunteered for the Armed Forces of Ukraine and headed to the front lines.

Valery Zaluzhny

Commander-in-Chief of the Armed Forces of Ukraine, military leader (Year of Birth: 1973).

A person who found themselves in the right place at the right time is the Chief of the General Staff of the Armed Forces of Ukraine, Valeriy Zaluzhny. For almost half a year, he has been doing what none of his predecessors did: waging a full-scale war against one of the most powerful armies in the world. And he's doing it well: the Kremlin dictator has not achieved any of his goals in Ukraine.

The Commander-in-Chief of the Armed Forces of Ukraine employs a maneuverable defense strategy, allowing for the containment of the enemy. He has succeeded in ensuring that local commanders have a certain degree of initiative. Furthermore, the current leadership of the Armed Forces of Ukraine is human-centric, with the well-being of civilians in the forefront of its priorities.

The American magazine Time included Zelensky in the list of the 100 most influential people in the world. In a profile about him in Politico, it is noted that he is a hero, not a star. In May, Volodymyr Zelensky made the Chief of the General Staff of the Armed Forces of Ukraine the first recipient of the Cross of Military Merit.

Vasyl Stuss

A poet, dissident

He was the face and voice of national resistance to the Soviet regime, sacrificing not only his literary career but also his life for the ideals of freedom and independence. For his acts of defiance and participation in protests, he spent a significant portion of his life in prisons and exile, where he continued his literary work. He passed away after declaring a hunger strike in prison.

Vyacheslav Chornovil

(1937-1999) was a political figure and dissident.
Viacheslav Chornovil was a prominent figure in the fearless Ukrainian dissident movement, the decades-long struggle of which culminated in the independence of Ukraine, officially affirmed through the Declaration of State Sovereignty and the Act of Proclamation of Independence. Chornovil, an activist in the national protest movement of the 1960s-1980s, spent many years in exile and prisons for his political convictions.

He became one of the founders of the Ukrainian Helsinki Union, as well as the party People's Movement of Ukraine, the first openly oppositional organizations to the Communist Party of the Soviet Union. He was a people's deputy in the early sessions of the Verkhovna Rada. He died in a car accident, and many still consider his death a political murder on the eve of the presidential elections in which he intended to participate.

Lina Kostenko

(B orn 1930), a Ukrainian poetess
The contemporary figure who has entered the realm of classics in Ukrainian literature is revered for her firm convictions and sharp words. Throughout her life, her work faced censorship in Soviet Ukraine as a result of her involvement in dissident activities. Surprisingly, this did not hinder her creative productivity; rather, it elevated Kostenko to a cult figure. During the Revolution of Dignity, Kostenko's patriotic verses served as inspiration for protest participants, who displayed them on banners and placards.

Today, her poem "Marusya Churai" is part of the school curriculum, and the prose novel "Notes of a Ukrainian Madman," released in 2010, became the best-selling book the following year, drawing crowds at literary readings. This year, the Ukrainian poetess received France's highest honor—the Order of the Legion of Honour.

Viktor Glushkov

(**1923**-1982) was a Ukrainian mathematician and cybernetician.

The first Ukrainian IT specialist, Viktor Glushkov, stood at the forefront of introducing computer technology into production. In the 1960s, he created and later organized the mass production of the first electronic computing machine in the USSR. In terms of characteristics and capabilities, it was on par with foreign counterparts. His developments ensured the operation of the largest plants in the country, including the Electron plant in Lviv and the Arsenal plant in Kyiv.

Glushkov's successes were known in the West, where he was referred to as the "god of Soviet cybernetics." He traveled around the world and even received invitations to continue his work in the United States, but he declined.

Mykola Amosov

(**1913**-2002) was a scientist and medical doctor. Cardiac surgeon with a global reputation revolutionized the world's scientific understanding of cardiovascular disease treatment. For the first time in the history of domestic medicine, he implanted a mitral heart valve, performed surgeries for cardiac defects, and pioneered the development and application of antithrombotic prostheses for heart valves. His methodology is widely used in global practice and has saved hundreds of thousands of lives. Additionally, Mykola Amosov authored several popular books.

Stepan Bandera

(1909-1959) a political figure.

He entered history as the leader of the independence movement in 20th-century Ukraine. Stepan Bandera was characterized not only by courage and dedication to ideals but also by radicalism. In retaliation for the Holodomor, he organized the assassination of the secretary of the Soviet consulate in Lviv. Additionally, in response to the persecution of Ukrainian peasants, he targeted the Minister of Internal Affairs of Poland.

In his efforts to defend Ukrainian sovereignty during the Second World War, Bandera considered as enemies those on different sides of the barricades, including the German occupiers and the Soviet authorities. The Germans sent him to camps for three years for declaring the Ukrainian state in the occupied city of Lviv. Additionally, both the Germans and Soviet special services made considerable efforts to capture and eliminate him. They succeeded in Munich after the war.

Roman Shukhevych

(1907-1950) was a military and political figure.

Roman Shukhevych, along with Stepan Bandera, became a powerful force in the struggle for the independence of Ukraine. He joined the Organization of Ukrainian Nationalists (OUN) as a young man, and in 1943, he became its leader, offering fierce resistance to both the German occupiers and Soviet authorities.

At the helm of the OUN (Organization of Ukrainian Nationalists), Shukhevych advocated for the consolidation of all nationalist movements in Ukraine. Through his efforts, the OUN adopted a program that essentially served as the program of the national liberation movement. In the 1930s, Shukhevych organized the first advertising company in Western Ukraine called "Fama" to financially support his activities and to support his family. The company became quite successful and transformed into a legal cover for the OUN's operations. Shukhevych was killed in 1950 near Lviv in a battle with a unit of Soviet special services.

Sergei Korolev

$\left(1907\right.$-1966) was a designer and the founder of astronautics.

Sergei Korolev is the Elon Musk of the 20th century: as a rocket engineer, he enabled humanity to explore space not just in theory but in practice. Under the careful guidance of this former prisoner of Stalin's camps (Korolev served time from 1938 to 1944), the first artificial satellite of Earth, Sputnik 1, orbited the planet. At the same time, the Soviet Union developed the first intercontinental ballistic missile.

Sergei Korolev, a key figure in the Soviet space program.

Sergei Korolev was born in Zhytomyr, Ukraine, and played a crucial role in the development of the Soviet space program. Under his leadership, the Soviet Union launched the first artificial satellite, Sputnik 1, in 1957, and later sent Yuri Gagarin into space aboard the Vostok 1 spacecraft in 1961.

Yuri Gagarin's historic spaceflight marked the first time a human orbited the Earth.

So, in summary, Yuri Gagarin was the cosmonaut who made the first manned spaceflight, and Sergei Korolev was the chief designer and engineer behind the Soviet space program.

Oleg Antonov

$($ **1906** -1984) was an aircraft designer.

Oleg Antonov became the chief designer for Soviet transport aviation, and under his leadership, a whole lineup of aircraft carrying the letters "An" on their fuselage was developed in the Soviet Union. Three giants held a special place among them—the An-22 Antei, An-124 Ruslan, and Mriya—the An-225, which emerged after his death, became the largest and most powerful cargo aircraft in the world. The Russian military destroyed the latter in February 2022 during the battles for Hostomel Airport.

Yuri Kondratyuk

(**1897**–1942) was a scientist and inventor, a pioneer in astronautics.

Yuri Kondratyuk was able to precisely ground the expression "to the Moon and back" – he was the first in the history of space exploration to calculate the optimal trajectory for a flight to Earth's natural satellite. The Apollo mission pioneers later utilized this "Kondratyuk's route," even naming one of the lunar craters after the Ukrainian scientist. Kondratyuk also contributed to the space industry with the principle of vertical rocket launches, the regulation of speed modes during ascent into the upper layers of the atmosphere, and the utilization of solar energy during flights. By the way, the scientist's real name is Alexander Shargei; he changed it after the October Bolshevik Revolution, as he had previously served as an officer in the White Army and feared reprisals.

Wilhelm Franz Habsburg-Lothringen

(**K**nown as Vasyl Vyshyvanyi), was a political and military figure. (1895–1948 or 1954)

The family of Austrian aristocrat Wilhelm Franz Habsburg-Lothringen not only ruled over Austria-Hungary but also directly descended from the Rurikids. In other words, Wilhelm traced his lineage back to the first princes of Kyivan Rus. As a member of the imperial family who received an excellent education and conversed in Italian during childhood, Archduke Wilhelm chose his national identity and advocated for the interests of Ukrainians in the Austro-Hungarian parliament, where he was elected by right of blood at the age of 21. After World War I, Wilhelm became the commander of the Ukrainian Sich Riflemen Legion. It was during this time that he acquired the new name Vasyl, further enriched by his enthusiasm for the traditional Ukrainian embroidered shirt, earning him the nickname "Vyshyvany" (Embroidered). Due to his pro-Ukrainian stance, Vyshyvany faced a dramatic fate: after World War II, he was effectively abducted from Vienna by Soviet intelligence services and tortured to death in Lukyanivska Prison.

Igor Sikorsky

One of the founding figures in world aviation, Igor Sikorsky, designed the legendary aircraft Grand and Ilya Muromets, pioneering heavy aviation construction. The revolutionary amphibious airplanes later invented by him were adopted by the United States. In 1919, he moved to America and founded Sikorsky Aircraft, which subsequently became a leading manufacturer of helicopter technology worldwide. Sikorsky is credited with creating 18 innovative helicopters and 17 airplanes, including those that accomplished the first-ever transcontinental passenger flights over the Atlantic and Pacific Oceans.89—1972 Aircraft designer, entrepreneur.

Oleksandr Bogomolets

(1881-1946) a Ukrainian scientist and pathophysiologist. His works have forever changed the global understanding of endocrinology, metabolic disorders, allergies, and even cancer. However, the primary among Alexander Bogomolets' fundamental discoveries is the study of connective tissue and the invention of its stimulating serum function, which is still used in medicine today. He also founded the first medical research institutions in the post-Soviet space—the Institute of Clinical Physiology and the Institute of Experimental Biology and Pathology.

Simon Petlyura

$($**1879**$-$1926), a political figure.

The classical revolutionary is remembered in history as the fearless chief ataman of the forces of the independent Ukrainian People's Republic (UNR) from May 1919 to November 1920 — the head of the Directory of the UNR. Additionally, he was a politician whose ideas and decisions still command respect, and in some cases, controversy. By the way, at birth, Petliura was given the name Semen, which he later changed, inspired by the activities of his Venezuelan counterpart, Simon Bolivar. Petliura's life was marked by highs and lows, victories and defeats, but the central idea of his life always remained the independence of Ukraine.

After his homeland fell into the hands of the Bolsheviks, he went to France, where he was involved in emigrant publications and, for the most part, posed no significant threat to Soviet authorities. However, in 1926, on a Paris street, he was shot by an agent of Soviet intelligence services.

Kazimir Malevich

(**1879**–1935), an artist.

Born in Kyiv, Kazimir Malevich is primarily known for creating an entire movement in visual arts – Suprematism. Emerging from the brush of the artist, who exclusively utilized flat geometric shapes in his works, came the quintessential example of abstract art – the Black Square.

Today, the works of this artist from a Ukrainian-Polish family adorn museums in New York and Berlin and remain coveted by the wealthiest art collectors. Yes, Malevich's painting "Suprematist Composition" was sold in 2018 for a fantastic $85 million.

Pavlo Skoropadsky

(**1873**–1945), a political figure.

Pavlo Skoropadsky, a nobleman and descendant of a renowned Cossack family, made a brilliant military career in the Russian Empire. He had the potential to become the founding father of an independent Ukrainian state. However, he played a complex political game, forming alliances with various factions active in Ukraine at the end of World War I. Ultimately, with the support of German occupation forces, he seized power and proclaimed himself the Hetman of Ukraine.

The rule of the hetman lasted no more than seven months. However, during this time, Skoropadsky made a significant contribution to the development of national science and culture: he founded the Academy of Sciences, the National Historical Museum and Library, established Ukrainian universities in Kyiv and Kamianets-Podilskyi, and founded 150 schools, providing them with several million Ukrainian textbooks. Under pressure from the forces of the Directory, Skoropadsky's regime fell, and he fled from Kyiv. Ultimately, the hetman found himself in Germany, where he perished towards the end of the Second World War.

Ivan Piddubny

(1871 –1949), a Ukrainian-born wrestler and athlete.

On the world wrestling stage, the name of the descendant of Cossacks, Ivan Piddubny, was associated with invincibility, endurance, and phenomenal technique for 40 years. The Poltava hero never lost any of the hundreds of matches he participated in and became the world champion in Greco-Roman wrestling six times. Competing in the heavyweight category at 118 kilograms, Piddubny was a proponent of fair competition, a favorite of the audience, and a symbol of true wrestling. He concluded his career at the age of 70 and spent the remaining years of his life in poverty, selling numerous awards for a livelihood.

Lesya Ukrainka

$($ **1871** –1913) was a Ukrainian poetess, writer, and playwright.

One of the most famous women in the history of Ukraine, Lesya Ukrainka (real name Larisa Kosach), suffered from a severe form of bone tuberculosis, yet despite this, she actively pursued her writing career and became a symbol of resilience. She wrote over a hundred poems, employing new forms and literary techniques. The stage adaptations of Ukrainka's dramatic poems, such as "The Stone Host," "Oblivion," and "Cassandra," are still part of the repertoire of Ukrainian theaters. Her drama-fairy tale "The Forest Song" has become a iconic element of the national culture. In addition to her poetic achievements, Ukrainka was also one of the finest translators in Ukrainian literature, adapting works by Heinrich Heine, Adam Mickiewicz, Victor Hugo, Homer, and other world classics for the Ukrainian readership.

Yevgeny Paton

$(1870$–1953), a Ukrainian scientist and engineer.

The Patons are the most famous dynasty of engineers and scientists in Ukraine. Its founder, Evgeny Paton, developed progressive methods for bridge design and implemented them in practice. In Kyiv, two of his works, the Parkovy Bridge and the bridge across the Dnieper River named after Paton himself, still function effectively. He also contributed to the advancement of welding technologies, a field later pursued by his son Boris. Boris made significant breakthroughs in welding technology, with one of the most noteworthy being the welding of living tissues. Additionally, Boris Paton served as the head of the National Academy of Sciences of Ukraine for almost 60 years until his death at the age of 101.

Mikhailo Grushevsky

(1866–1934), a Ukrainian historian and politician.

Mikhailo Hrushevsky is an example of the assertion that a talented individual can be successful in multiple fields. Primarily, he is the founder of Ukrainian scientific historiography and the author of the first comprehensive study, "History of Ukraine-Rus." In total, he wrote over 2,000 scholarly works. Although his contributions to history are significant, it is noteworthy that in the early 20th century, Hrushevsky led the Central Rada of the Ukrainian People's Republic (UNR), worked on the project of the Constitution of independent Ukraine, and signed the Universal Declaration of Independence.

Vladislav Gorodetsky

(1863 –1930), an architect."
Vladyslav Horodetsky, of Polish origin, spent the most fruitful 30 years of his creative career in the Ukrainian capital and even held the position of city architect. He became the author of iconic buildings in Kyiv, including the House with Chimeras on Bankova Street, the Church of St. Nicholas, and the National Bank building. For these works, Horodetsky earned the nickname "Kyiv's Gaudi." He possessed not only the imagination of a creator but also the talent of an entrepreneur: Horodetsky owned the For cement plant and implemented his architectural solutions primarily using monolithic concrete structures.

Shalom Aleichem

(**1859**–1916) ,a Yiddish writer and humorist.

Solomon Rabinovich, born in Pereyaslav, a city in the Kyiv region, became a central figure in the global Jewish enlightenment movement. Thanks to his creative work, the man who adopted the greeting pseudonym "peace be with you" (in Yiddish – Sholom-Aleichem) became a pioneer of modern Yiddish literature. The combination of the life dramas of ordinary people and sparkling humor made Sholom-Aleichem popular worldwide. During his lifetime, he traveled extensively throughout Europe and performed before admirers in Geneva, London, Berlin, and Warsaw. Today, 10 of his major novels, 20 plays, and hundreds of short stories have been translated into many languages.

Ivan Franko

(1856-1916), a Ukrainian writer and publicist.

Ivan Franko was the first Ukrainian writer who managed to earn his livelihood through his craft while still alive. His literary legacy, accumulated over 40 years of work, is impressive: it includes several thousand works in Ukrainian, Polish, German, Bulgarian, Czech, and Russian languages. The 100 volumes of Franko's works encompass poetry, prose, scripts, early translations of Dante and Shakespeare, reviews, and scholarly works in the fields of literature and ethnography.

The literary contribution of the Ukrainian writer was so significant that in 1916, he became the first and so far the only known Ukrainian poet to be nominated for the Nobel Prize in Literature. Whether he would have received it or not remains unanswered and will never be known: in May of the same year, Franko passed away.

Ilya Mechnikov

(**1845**–1916), a prominent Ukrainian-born biologist. The Nobel laureate in the field of physiology or medicine, Ilya Mechnikov, gained recognition in scientific circles for his research on immunity. He was the first to introduce the concept of phagocytosis, the process by which cells of an organism engulf foreign particles and solid materials. Mechnikov was also deeply interested in the processes of birth and aging, and he is considered one of the main proponents of evolutionary embryology and gerontology.

Despite his brilliant scientific career, Mechnikov often faced criticism from colleagues in his homeland who faulted him for lacking a formal medical education. Eventually, at the personal invitation of Louis Pasteur, Mechnikov moved to Paris, where he spent 28 years leading a laboratory at the Pasteur Institute.

Mykola Leontovych

A Ukrainian composer, conductor, ethnomusicologist, and teacher. Mykola Leontovich was born on December 13, 1877, in the family of a rural priest, Father Dmytro, in the village of Monastyrok, now in the Nemirivsky district. He would later become a renowned composer and singer, known globally. In the history of world musical art, Leontovych is recognized as the author of artistic arrangements for choir based on Ukrainian folk songs, numbering around 200. Additionally, he is celebrated as the creator of a refined choral miniature genre, utilizing the texts and melodies of folk songs.

Among his best-known arrangements of folk songs, distinguished by their melodiousness, are "Shchedryk, (Coral of the bells)" "Dudaryk," "Pralia," "Kozaka nesut," "Piyut pivni," "Oi, za-zha hory kam'yanoyi," "Zhenchykok-brenchychok," "Zashumila lishchynonka," and others.

"Schedryk" is known all over the world. Just what you here on Christmas.

Taras Shevchenko

(1814–1861), a Ukrainian poet, prose writer, and artist. One of the most famous Ukrainians in history, often referred to today as a national genius, is Taras Shevchenko. Despite spending most of his life in Russia and writing some of his works in the Russian language, the central theme of Shevchenko's creativity revolves around social inequality in Ukraine, the oppression of the people, and the restrictions imposed by authority on their freedom. Today, Shevchenko is one of the most widely published authors worldwide. His collection "Kobzar" has been translated into over a hundred languages, and more than 1,300 monuments to the poet are erected in 35 countries. This is the largest number of monuments dedicated to a cultural figure anywhere in the world.

Mykola Pirogov

$($ **1810** -1881), a Ukrainian and Russian surgeon, anatomist, and professor.

Nikolai Pirogov's contribution to the development and shaping of medicine is difficult to overestimate. He played a crucial role in creating the first atlas of topographic anatomy in humans. Pirogov was the first to use ether anesthesia during operations in field conditions and essentially established the institute of military field surgeons in its modern sense. Thanks to Pirogov's innovations, surgeons began amputating limbs with minimal losses, and overall, operations became less traumatic for patients.

Born in Moscow, Pirogov lived in Ukraine for 30 years. Throughout these years, alongside his private practice, he devoted two days a week to providing free medical care to the poor. He was the first in the history of world medicine to apply plaster casts for fractures and introduced the current methodology of medical sorting of the wounded during combat operations.

Mykola Gogol

(**1809**-1852), a Ukrainian and Russian-language writer and playwright.

The classic born in Sorochyntsi who wrote in Russian, infused Ukrainian literature with mysticism, humor, and romantic folklore. One of the peaks of this direction in his work is considered the famous "Evenings on a Farm near Dikanka." Another merit of Gogol is his keen attention to sharp social themes that have remained relevant for two centuries. Using his favorite tool, satire, in "The Government Inspector" and "Dead Souls," Gogol mocked the vices of society, including narrow-mindedness and corruption.

Kyrylo Rozumovsky

(1728 –1803) was a Hetman. The younger brother of the favorite of Empress Yelizaveta Petrovna is remembered in history as the last hetman of the Zaporozhian Cossacks, a status that Elizabeth reinstated specifically for him. On the other hand, Rozumovsky undertook the reorganization of the Zaporozhian Cossack Host, promoting not only military skills but also historical education. He built extensively in the hetmanate capitals of Baturyn and Hlukhiv, even bringing Italian opera and French theater to these cities.

Despite his fondness for St. Petersburg and his status as the wealthiest landowner in Ukraine, Razumovsky was captivated by reforms and the revival of Cossack culture during his time. Under his influence, the Cossacks regained many freedoms. A notable aspect of the Ukrainian's biography is his leadership of the Russian Academy of Sciences, which he headed for 43 years, and his patronage of many distinguished scholars, including Mikhail Lomonosov.

Grigory Skovoroda

(1722-1794) was a Ukrainian philosopher and writer. He is commonly referred to as the father of Ukrainian philosophical thought. By adapting the works of ancient Greek thinkers to Ukrainian realities and incorporating their foundations into the academic education system, Hryhorii Skovoroda had a profound impact on both his contemporaries and subsequent generations. His works are dedicated to the fundamental concepts of inequality, freedom, and the search for purpose. Skovoroda's reflections inspired him to embark on journeys, and he traveled throughout Ukraine and Europe. In addition to serious philosophical treatises, many works of lighter genres with equally profound content flowed from his pen.

Petro Kalnyshevsky, The last hetman of the Zaporizhian Host

Petro Kalnyshevsky w,s born around 1708 and died in 1775.

The last hetman of the Zaporizhian Host entered history as a defender of the territorial possessions and rights of the Zaporizhian Sich, earning boundless popular love for his actions. Despite the will of Russian Empress Catherine II, who removed him from office, the elders repeatedly elected him as hetman for a period of 10 years. During this time, Kalnyshevsky proved himself as a strong leader, promoting agriculture and trade, refusing to surrender runaway peasants to landowners, and sponsoring the construction of churches.

This Muscovite throne seemed insufficient, and ultimately, due to the machinations of Prince Grigory Potemkin, the last hetman was forced to surrender the Sich without a fight and ended his life in exile at the Solovetsky Monastery.

Pylyp Orlyk (1672-1742) was a political figure and hetman.

The successor to Ivan Mazepa, in his attempts to retain the hetmanate after Mazepa's death, created one of the most significant documents in Ukrainian history—the first draft of the Constitution. To secure the support of the Cossacks during the formation of an alliance with Sweden, Orlyk signed a series of laws, treaties, and resolutions that regulated the subordination between hetmans and starshynas, significantly reducing the powers of the hetman. He was a supporter of European integration and a staunch advocate for the liberation of Ukrainian lands from Moscow, which later forced him to flee to Europe. There, he continued to seek support for Ukrainian statehood by issuing manifestos to the rulers of France, England, Saxony, the Vatican, and Prussia.

Ivan Mazepa

(**1639**-1709), a military and political figure, a hetman. The long-living hetman not only united Left Bank and Right Bank Ukraine under his leadership but also ruled various territories for a total of 22 years. Forced to engage in delicate diplomatic maneuvers to preserve the integrity of Ukraine, Mazepa sought support even from sworn enemies. He found himself under the patronage of the Moscow Tsar Peter I at times and expressed support for the Swedish Empire, which was at war with him. Mazepa made an invaluable contribution to the cultural development of Ukraine. About 200 cathedrals in the Ukrainian Baroque style were constructed using the hetman's treasury, and Kyiv-Mohyla Collegium was elevated to the status of an academy with the addition of several new buildings. His poetic attempts, such as the song "Duma," have also survived to the present day and are considered a valuable heritage of Ukrainian socio-political thought from that time.

Petro Mohyla

A prominent Ukrainian Orthodox clergyman and statesman who lived from 1597 to 1647.

He is best known for his contributions to the Orthodox Church and his role in the cultural and educational development of Ukraine during the 17th century. Mogila was a key figure in the Orthodox Church, serving as the Metropolitan of Kyiv and Halych, and he played a crucial role in the establishment of the Kyiv Mohyla Academy.

The son of the ruler of Moldova received the nickname "Movile" at birth, and he later became known as Mogila in Ukraine, where his family sought refuge from persecution in their homeland. Having received a prestigious European education, Mogila made a career in the clergy in Ukraine, first becoming the archimandrite of the Kyiv-Pechersk Lavra and later the Kyiv Metropolitan. Through Mogila's efforts, the Polish king essentially legitimized Orthodoxy in Kyiv, allowing the construction of churches, appointment of officials, and the practice of sacraments.

However, Mogila's main achievement was the establishment of the Kyiv-Mohyla Collegium, which has persisted to this day as the Kyiv-Mohyla Academy. It is considered one of the oldest and most prestigious higher education institutions in Eastern Europe.

Bohdan Khmelnytsky

(1596–1657) was a military and political leader, hetman. Bohdan Khmelnytsky was one of the key figures in the progress of Ukrainian history. Driven by the idea of separating the western and central lands of modern Ukraine from the Polish-Lithuanian Commonwealth, he led the first successful Cossack uprising and became the first hetman of the subsequently formed Ukrainian state known as Hetmanate. In addition to his reputation as a brave military general, Khmelnytsky was also recognized as a skilled diplomat. In order to permanently repel Polish attacks, he orchestrated three coalitions consecutively—the Crimean-Ottoman, Moscow, and Swedish. While these coalitions did not achieve the desired effect, they solidified Khmelnytsky's status as a talented negotiator.

The talented Ukrainian military leader who entered history as the ideologist of the Cossacks is Bohdan Khmelnytsky. Under his leadership, the Cossacks transcended the narrow confines of local communities and actively participated in the political life of the state. During the time of Khmelnytsky, the Cossacks transformed into a semblance of a regular army, with the establishment of divisions into regiments and hundreds, organized military training, and the influx of fresh recruits, including peasants.

Khmelnytsky became renowned as a harsh but effective leader. He prohibited the consumption of alcohol during military campaigns, expelled or punished with death those who violated discipline. His reforms contributed to military successes, particularly in campaigns against the Crimean Khanate, the Ottoman Empire, and the Moscow Tsardom on the side of the Polish-Lithuanian Commonwealth.

Due to these victories, Khmelnytsky earned a good reputation with the Polish king, which briefly allowed him to secure a form of autonomy for Ukraine.

Petro Konashevich-Sahaidachny

(Circa 1577 – 1622), a military and political figure, a hetman.

The talented Ukrainian military leader who entered history as the ideologist of the Cossacks is Bohdan Khmelnytsky. Under his leadership, the Cossacks expanded beyond the narrow confines of local communities and actively participated in the political life of the state. During the time of Khmelnytsky, the Cossacks transformed into a semblance of a regular army, with the establishment of divisions into regiments and companies, and the organization of military training, including the influx of recruits, including peasants.

Khmelnytsky gained fame as a stern but effective administrator. He prohibited the consumption of alcohol during campaigns, expelled or imposed severe punishments for offenses within the military ranks. His reforms contributed to military successes, particularly in campaigns against the Crimean Khanate, the Ottoman Empire, and the Tsardom of Muscovy on the side of the Polish-Lithuanian Commonwealth.

Due to these victories, Khmelnytsky earned a favorable reputation with the Polish king, which briefly allowed him to secure a form of autonomy for Ukraine.

Dmytro (Baida) Vishnevetsky

(Circa 1517 – circa 1563/1564), a military and political figure, a hetman.

The princely title and belonging to a noble family of Ukrainian-Lithuanian magnates did not prevent Vyshnevetsky from becoming the forefather of the Ukrainian Cossacks. On the contrary, thanks to his lineage, in 1551 Vyshnevetsky was appointed the starosta (military commander) of the city-fortresses of Cherkasy and Kaniv. Just a few years later, he privately erected a fortress on the island of Malaya Khortytsya. Historians believe that this fortress became the prototype of the Zaporizhian Sich and the main outpost of the Cossacks in the struggle against aggressors.

Vyshnevetsky gained particular fame for his diplomatic skills. During his active career, he managed to establish relations with leaders from the Ottoman Empire, Poland, and Moscow.

Konstantin and Konstantin-Vasil Ostrogski

(1460-1530 and 1526-1608), military and state figures, as well as patrons.

The Ostrih family became prominent in history primarily through the efforts of its younger member, Kostiantyn-Vasyl, who established the first classical university in Eastern Europe—the Ostroh Academy. Within its walls, descendants of the distinguished Ukrainian-Lithuanian family gathered eminent minds of the time, organized a library, and, with the help of the printer Ivan Fedorov, enriched it with 20 new publications. Vasyl's philanthropic pursuits were influenced by his father, the renowned military commander of the 16th century and Grand Hetman of Lithuania, Kostiantyn Ostrih. The latter engaged in 35 battles against the Tatars and the Moscow state, losing only two.

Despite his service in Catholic Lithuania, the military commander did a lot for Ukrainian Orthodoxy: he defended the church's right to autonomy and built Orthodox churches in honor of each of his victories. Ostrog owned 100 cities, 1,300 villages, and 40 castles, and being one of the richest people of his time, he collected huge donations for the less fortunate. From the income of his lands, which amounted to about a million zlotys annually, his son Kostiantyn-Vasyl later founded the Ostroh Academy.

Danilo Romanovich Halytskyi

(Circa 1201/1204 — 1264), a ruler of the Galicia-Volhynia Principality.

The rule of Prince Danylo was marked by an unprecedented economic and cultural upswing in the western regions of Ukraine. Despite external challenges such as Mongol-Tatar invasions and other geopolitical crises, he emerged as a subtle and sophisticated politician. The Ukrainian prince forged alliances with Rome, the Teutonic Order, Poles, and Hungarians. As a result of these agreements, Danylo was crowned, and the Galician-Volhynian state, strengthened by him, became a powerful successor to the Kyivan Rus and endured in this status for 150 years.

Nestor the Chronicler (circa 1056–1114) was a monk of the Kyiv Pechersk Lavra monastery.

Nestor can be considered the first renowned journalist and intellectual of Kyivan Rus. As an Orthodox monk, he impeccably mastered the Greek language, had a good understanding of history and literature, but most importantly, he is credited with authorship of the unique historical source of that period, "The Tale of Bygone Years" (also known as the Primary Chronicle). It is believed that Nestor not only detailed current events but, through the examination of other manuscripts, reconstructed and documented important historical milestones. For his contributions, Nestor the Chronicler is revered among the saints in the Roman Catholic Church.

Anna Yaroslavovna

(Circa 1032/1036 – circa 1075/1089), a Kyivan princess and Queen of France.

The youngest of the three daughters of Kyivan Prince Yaroslav the Wise not only successfully married the French King Henry I but also managed to become a prominent political figure, influencing both foreign and domestic policies in France. Anna had a good reputation with the Pope, engaging in correspondence with the Holy See, and she gifted France with two sons – the future King Philip I and Count Hugh, a leader in the First Crusade. Anna Yaroslavna even impacted the daily life of the French: as an educated and worldly Kyivan princess, she contributed to the spread of literacy and the improvement of domestic culture, particularly promoting certain personal hygiene practices.

Yaroslav the Wise

(C. 978 – 1054), the Grand Prince of Kiev.

Yaroslav the Wise could be described as a reformer and a Euro-optimist today. Under his rule, Kyivan Rus reached the highest level of development and became a powerful European state of that time. In addition to numerous victories over nomadic tribes and other hostile groups, Yaroslav transformed Rus into a legal state by issuing the official code of laws known as the Ruska Pravda. Yaroslav himself bestowed two architectural gems upon Kyiv – the Saint Sophia Cathedral and the Golden Gate.

As a secular and highly educated individual, he founded schools and libraries, initiated the translation of Greek books, established a system of hereditary succession to the throne, and strengthened relations with the West through marital alliances for his daughters.

Volodymyr the Great

(Circa 956/958 – 1015), the Grand Prince of Kiev. Olga's grandson continued her legacy and permanently inscribed his name in history as a ruler who introduced Christianity to his territories. Additionally, at his initiative, the cities of Pereyaslav and Volodymyr-Volynsky emerged on the map. Under his command, the Desyatynna Church was erected in Kyiv, and the state minted its first gold coins. Modern Ukrainians can also thank him for the national coat of arms—Volodymyr was the first to use the trident as his personal emblem.

Olga

(C. 910–969), the Grand Princess of Kyiv.

Princess Olga, one of the most prominent figures in Ukrainian history, exemplified through her own actions how a strong female hand could bring order to an entire state. After the death of her husband, Prince Igor, she had to take control of the government in place of her underage son Svyatoslav. During the 15 years of Olga's rule, she transformed Rus into an organized territorial unit. Through her efforts, a system of tax collection was established, and the country saw the introduction of territorial-administrative divisions and even a judiciary.

The princess was active in foreign policy and gained renown among her contemporaries as an intelligent and powerful leader. Additionally, Olga was one of the first rulers of Kievan Rus to embrace Christianity.

Chapter Fifteen
Echoes of Eternity - A Tapestry of History

As the golden sun dipped below the horizon, casting its warm hues upon the vast Ukrainian landscape, the ancient land whispered its tales to those who listened with eager hearts. The final chapter of Ukraine's story unfolded, a narrative woven with threads of legends, truths, and the resilient spirit of a people bound by a shared love for their enchanting homeland. A Symphony of Nature's Splendor Ukraine, with its fertile plains and majestic Carpathian Mountains, stood as a testament to nature's opulence. The Dnipro River, winding gracefully through the heart of the country, mirrored the resilience of the Ukrainian spirit, reflecting both the tumultuous past and the promise of a vibrant future. The picturesque landscapes painted an inviting canvas, inviting travelers to delve into a world where myth and reality intertwined.

In the glow of twilight, as fireflies danced around ancient oaks, the whispering winds carried the echoes of Cossack tales and folklore. Legends spoke of the mystical creatures that once roamed the dense forests and the mystical energy that emanated from the sacred land. From the bewitching beauty of the Carpathians to the endless fields of golden wheat swaying like a sea under the azure sky, Ukraine's natural wonders beckoned all who sought solace in the embrace of Mother Nature.

A Tapestry of History

Ukraine, a crucible of civilizations, bore the indelible marks of centuries past. The cobblestone streets of Lviv echoed with the footsteps of poets and philosophers, while the ancient churches of Kyiv stood as silent witnesses to the enduring faith of the Ukrainian people. Each stone in the castle walls held a tale of triumph and struggle, creating a tapestry of history that unfolded like a cherished manuscript.

The heritage of Ukraine was not merely confined to its museums and monuments; it pulsed through the veins of its people. From the fervor of the Kievan Rus to the trials of the Holodomor, the chapters of Ukraine's chronicle painted a resilient portrait of a nation that refused to be silenced. The struggles only fueled the desire for a future where the echoes of the past would resonate with the promise of freedom.

Cultural Kaleidoscope

Ukraine's culture, a rich mosaic of traditions, music, and dance, captivated the imagination of those who sought to explore its depths. The spirited melodies of the bandura echoed through the cobblestone streets, inviting all to join the dance of life. The vibrant colors of vyshyvanka embroidered tales of unity and identity, proclaiming the pride of a nation that refused to be subdued.

In the heart of Kyiv, where the past and present converged, the golden domes of St. Sophia's Cathedral soared towards the heavens. Beneath the shadows of those sacred spires, Ukrainians gathered to celebrate their heritage, forging bonds that transcended time and adversity. It was in these moments of shared joy and solemn reflection that the true essence of Ukrainian culture revealed itself — a resilient spirit unyielding in the face of external forces.

Ukrainian cuisine, with its hearty and flavorful dishes, is another facet of the nation's cultural identity. Borscht, pierogi, and varenyky are not just meals; they are culinary expressions of a people whose history is deeply intertwined with the fertile lands they cultivate.

The warmth of Ukrainian hospitality is perhaps most evident in the lively celebrations and communal gatherings that punctuate daily life. Whether it be a family feast or a village festival, Ukrainians embrace the joy of shared moments, fostering a sense of community that transcends borders.

The Struggle for Independence

As the winds of change swept across the Ukrainian steppes, the nation found itself at a crossroads. The struggle for independence, a recurring theme in Ukraine's narrative, resonated with renewed vigor. The people, like the heroes of old, stood united against the currents of adversity, their gaze fixed on the horizon of a sovereign future.

In the city squares and village gatherings, the spirit of the Orange Revolution and the Euromaidan protests lingered, symbols of a collective yearning for self-determination. The echoes of "Slava Ukraini!" (Glory to Ukraine!) reverberated, not as a mere slogan but as a declaration of an unyielding spirit that refused to be extinguished.

In conclusion, Ukraine beckons with a magnetic charm that extends far beyond its struggle for independence. Its allure lies not only in the breathtaking landscapes and vibrant cultural tapestry but also in the resilient spirit of its people. As we turn the final page, let us carry with us the image of Ukraine as a nation that has not only survived the trials of history but has emerged as a testament to the enduring power of freedom, beauty, and cultural richness.

Don't miss out!

Visit the website below and you can sign up to receive emails whenever Olga Bandura publishes a new book. There's no charge and no obligation.

https://books2read.com/r/B-A-JYFCB-GYMSC

BOOKS 2 READ

Connecting independent readers to independent writers.

About the Author

I am a Ukrainian. I am an artist and I try myself as a writer. I like Ukraine, its nature, people. I have a summer house in a beautiful land here with a lake and hills, wild animals.

I like communicating with people all around the world. Tell me how are you.